Kidwheels

Understanding the Child in the Chart

Cornelia Hansen

The Wessex Astrologer Ltd

Published in 2018 by
The Wessex Astrologer Ltd
PO Box 9307
Swanage
BH19 9BF

For a full list of our titles go to www.wessexastrologer.com

© Cornelia Hansen 2018

Cornelia Hansen asserts the moral right to be recognised as
the author of this work

Cover Design by Jonathan Taylor

A catalogue record for this book is available at The British Library

ISBN 9781910531310

No part of this book may be reproduced or used in any form or
by any means without the written permission of the publisher. A
reviewer may quote brief passages.

Contents

Preface	vii
Introduction	xi

Chapter 1
Temperament and Quality of Mood — 1

Chapter 2
Approach/Withdrawal and Adaptability — 11

Chapter 3
Intensity of Reaction and Threshold of Response — 19

Chapter 4
Distractibility and Persistence — 30

Chapter 5
Activity Level — 42

Chapter 6
Temperamental Types — 56

Chapter 7
Goodness of Fit and the Parental Axis — 70

Chapter 8
Parenting Issues — 86

Chapter 9
Concluding Thoughts — 98

Appendices
Appendix A: Parent Questionnaire   103
Appendix B: Student Observations   107
Appendix C: Worksheets   108
Appendix D: Temperament Assessment Scale   115

Bibliography   117

For

Karen, David, Eric, and Alan

and my grandson Samuel

Preface

"There is no single effort more radical in its potential for saving the world than a transformation of the way we raise our children."
Marianne Williamson

The original seed for this book was planted in my head in the 1970s when I was working on a Master's Degree in Child Development. I was introduced to a longitudinal study done in the Fifties on temperament in children, which intrigued me. At the same time, I was studying astrology with Joan McEvers and Marion March at Aquarius Workshops. The idea came to me that somehow I might be able to connect the child development study to astrology. After all, hadn't the concept of temperament been with us from ancient times? Isn't it still part of analyzing someone's natal chart? Working as a teacher for the Los Angeles Early Education Centers gave me the opportune place to begin research with my class of more than forty preschoolers. I outlined my plan, presented it to my supervisor, then the Child Development Division, and was given the permission to proceed.

Behind the commitment to doing this study were two deep desires that motivated me: one concerned the need to be able to help parents to better understand the child in their care. My belief and experience by this time led me to consider each child as unique and in need of special management. As a mother of four, I learned that each child in the family was different from his or her sibling. Most mothers are aware of this but, like me, had difficulty explaining *why*. I wanted to know why. Why were some children succeeding and others not? Why did some children develop behavior problems and others did not? Was anyone at fault? If so, who? And most importantly, was there any way to ensure a child's successful development?

The second desire of mine came from astrology itself. I pored over astrology books and articles but failed to find the answers to my questions. There were not enough astrological books on children at that time. I felt more studies were needed, especially some based on a semblance of the scientific model. I had just completed a research project on creativity in kindergarten children at the California State University at Northridge (CSUN). Since it was quite successful, I now felt ready to attempt researching temperament and how it could be determined in the natal charts of the children in my care. I wanted to find a way to be able to understand the child in a special way that was not just a watered-down version of adult interpretation. In addition, any reading of an adult's chart, I thought, can be illuminated by knowing the inner child of that adult.

During my twenty-five years at the children's center, I was able to complete a second Master's Degree in Clinical Psychology at Antioch University, and an internship at the YMCA Counseling Center. During my internship, I conducted "Mommy and Me" workshops with toddlers and taught parenting classes for court-appointed "abusive" mothers. Some of my clients included adolescents with a variety of behavioral problems. At times I was able to use my astrological skills to illuminate my cases. Once I received my license as a Marriage, Family, Child Therapist and began practice, I continued to work with children of diverse ages with a large range of problems from sexual and alcohol abuse to phobias, school problems, and the effects of parental divorce. My work with whole families gave me additional insight into family dynamics.

During the Nineties I was able to share some of the results with other professionals in a regular column called "Kidwheels" in the magazine *Aspects*, published by Aquarius Workshops. I also contributed a chapter, "Child and Parent," to the book *Web of Relationships*, edited by Joan McEvers and published by Llewellyn (1992).

I have continued to add to, refine and use my methods until the present day. After leaving the children's center, I spent nine years teaching English, Psychology and Humanities to 9th through 12th grade in high school. This gave me a great opportunity to study adolescents and their development at first hand. It also gave me insight into the need for the education system to incorporate concepts of temperament into teacher training. Differences in temperament have a strong connection to whether the child has a successful school experience or not.

On looking back, it seems as if my whole life of personal experience, education, astrological studies, plus work as a teacher and therapist have now led me to this final project; putting it all together in a book. In fact, one book may not be enough. I'm already taking notes for a second volume on stages of development through the house polarities and a third on counseling with parents. At this point, I must give credit to Bruce Scofeld for his wonderful book *Circuitry of the Self* (2001) which acted as an inspiration for me to get to work. He clearly and accurately connected astrology to the developmental model and called for further testing on this subject. His model of stages of development being initiated by planetary returns helped expand my views on this subject.

Last, but most importantly, I want to thank my dear friend, Karen McCauley, who has encouraged me from the beginning of this work since we met in Aquarius Workshops many years ago. Without her, this book probably would not have been written.

Cornelia Hansen, 2018

Introduction

"Being alert to temperamental differences and understanding how they require different caregiving approaches are crucial to nurturing children's healthy emotional growth."

Stella Chess

The modern concept of temperament as being the cause of individual differences which appear at birth and continue over time has been widely accepted in the field of child development. It appears in every child development textbook. The seminal work was a longitudinal study developed by a team of researchers, Alexander Thomas, M.D., Stella Birch, M.D., two psychiatrists, and a pediatrics research professor, Herbert G. Birch. The team began with eighty families contributing 141 infants to the study. Their results were published in *Temperament and Behavior Disorders in Children* (1968). The team continued to follow these children through adolescence into young adulthood and to publish their results. This original study has been the impetus for much research and longitudinal studies by others. Widely accepted now is the idea that a child's development and behavior come about through the continual interaction of the child's temperament and the environment. In other words, development is bi-directional and interactive, not subject to just nature or nurture. Nor is it determined by early or late experience; all have a role to play as development continues from childhood through adulthood and into old age. In addition, Piaget's concept of intellectual development occurring through distinct stages rather than from a gradual learning curve has been verified by recent brain research. The importance of Erick Erikson's work in social/emotional stages of development also holds a high place in the field.

Definition of Temperament

Stated by Thomas, Chess and Birch (1968, p.4) "Temperament is the behavioral style of the individual child – the HOW rather than the WHAT (abilities and content) or WHY (motivations) of behavior". It describes the "characteristic tempo, rhythmicity, adaptability, energy expenditure, mood, and focus of a child, independently of the content of any specific behavior."

Other developmentalists have contributed to the above definition. Kagan (1989) spent twenty-five years studying infants for two temperamental types which he called high-reactive or inhibited (most likely to become shy or timid) and low-reactive or uninhibited, more likely to be "bold and sociable". Others have emphasized dimensions of "emotionality, activity and sociability" (Buss and Plomin,1975) or "reactivity and self-regulation" (Rothbart, 1989). What all researchers generally agree on is that temperament is rooted in biology, is present at birth, and is stable over time and across various situations.

Newer research has studied the effects of temperament on school functioning (Keogh, 2003), demonstrating that temperament contributes to whether or not the child will be successful in school. Another aspect to research has been to develop parent training programs to familiarize parents with the temperament of their child and how to adapt their management to fit the child's needs. All the research on temperament has produced a number of books, articles and websites to help educate the public.

Overview of the Temperamental Model

Now, the question is (I hear you asking) what has all this to do with astrology and reading a child's chart? The answer lies within the chapters of this book. As stated before, my project was based on the work of Thomas, Chess and Birch and their definition of temperament. It also includes their concept of "the goodness of fit" model. What follows is a brief review of their findings which will be described in greater depth in later chapters.

Thomas, Chess and Birch established nine categories of responses that were reliably scored on a three-point scale of low-medium-high. These were as follows:

1. Level of motor activity
2. Approach/withdrawal to new persons or experience
3. Threshold of sensitivity to stimuli
4. Energy level or intensity of response
5. General mood (positive or negative)
6. Degree of distractibility from a task
7. Attention span and persistence
8. Adaptability to changes in environment
9. Regularity of body functions (this is one element I did not explore)

Some of these characteristics were found to cluster together in patterns to produce "Temperamental Types" such as "Easy children" (40 percent of the sample), "Slow-to-warm-up children" (15-20 percent) and "Difficult Children" (10 percent). The remaining 35 percent represented various combinations of traits.

The "goodness of fit" model has been widely accepted in child development circles. It refers to the match between the child's temperament and his physical and social environment. When the demands of the environment are in accord with the child's own characteristics ("good fit"), development proceeds in a progressive manner. With a "poor fit" (resulting from a stressful interaction with the environment), development proceeds with difficulty. Certain temperamental patterns were more vulnerable to developing behavior problems.

Armed with these concepts of temperament, temperamental types and the "goodness of fit" model, I proceeded to plan how I would conduct my research into discovering a connection between the horoscopes of children and their temperament. Could a child's natal chart tell me his or her temperamental type and whether or not it fit into the environment (s)he was born into?

Sample Group

The initial group of children to be studied was forty-six, aged two to four years. The group included a variety of children who were white, black, Hispanic, Indian, and Asian. The majority of families at the Center came from a low socioeconomic class since the purpose of the Center was to provide child care for poor, working mothers. Since temperament is rooted in biology and is universal, I did not consider this a problem in selecting my sample. Also, every child was required to have a birth certificate on file at the Center so I was able to confirm the date, time and place of birth of every child.

Step one was to get permission to conduct the study. I presented my proposal to my supervisor who passed it on to the Child Development Division of the Los Angeles Unified School District for approval. It was granted.

Step two was to gain permission from the parents of the children in my class to carry out my study. I created a parent survey (found in Appendix A) which requested general information about the family, health history of the child, form of discipline used at home, habits, fears, birth data and birth order. Questions related to each temperamental characteristic were developed using the Thomas, Chess and Birch model. Parents were asked to rate the child as high, variable, or low on each one. I wrote a letter to each parent asking them to grant permission for the study by turning in the completed survey. All of them did.

Step three was to construct a birth chart for each child. All the surveys and birth charts were collected together and set aside for later examination.

Step four was to develop Observation Sheets (see Appendix B) which would be used by myself and the staff, consisting of another teacher and three teacher aides. It should be noted that all of the staff were well-trained in making and recording observations of children already. After familiarizing the staff on the concepts of each temperamental component, such as activity level, they were given the observation sheet with the class list to rate the children they worked with, as well as make comments on what they observed. At staff meetings we also were able to discuss their observations. The classroom was divided into several learning centers and each staff member was assigned to a different center for a period of a week. The same was true for the outside play area. Over time, this procedure gave all of us an opportunity to observe multiple children during the various activities of the day. Observations extended to group activities, mealtimes and entering and exiting the school. Each staff member was assigned a group of eight to ten children they met with daily for small group time and meals. This allowed them to develop closer relationships with and greater knowledge of the children in their group. The input they gave me was extremely helpful to the project. Since we saw the mothers every day and had frequent conferences with them, it gave me a good perspective on the mother's (or father's) interaction with their child. We were also required to bi-annually complete developmental progress reports on each child for the district and discuss these with the parents. The reports gave me a resource for additional information. The collection of data continued for months until each child had been observed and graded on each temperamental trait.

Analyzing the Data

Once all the data had been collected, I began to examine the charts of the children for connections to the observations. This procedure entailed selecting a temperamental trait, such as activity level, listing the children who had been listed as high, medium and low. Examining the charts of all the children in the high group, I looked for astrological elements they had in common, giving numerical weights to each according to the frequency they occurred. To give one example, I found children who demonstrated high activity frequently had Mars in Sagittarius or Mars aspected to Jupiter as one indication. The same procedure was followed for every category of every temperamental component. I developed what I called a "signature" of astrological factors that described each level of a temperamental trait.

In Addition

I continued to study children at the Center through the Eighties and Nineties, observing their behavior and examining their charts for these signatures. I also added charts from my private practice, my friends, and charts of my children and my grandson. The final number of charts gathered totalled 125. Over the years, I have been able to develop and refine my system. I created a numerical method to make it easier to determine the signatures for each component of temperament and a scale to measure them. Although I have followed the model described by Thomas, Chess and Birch, I cannot claim any strategy of qualitative analysis on the data. Also, the sample size is not by any means large enough to be called scientific. I also don't wish to claim that my system is the only way to measure temperament; it's a different way, based on modern concepts of temperament found in the field of child development.

Astrologers have long recognized the significance of the elements and modalities for describing temperament. The idea of the elements, Fire, Air, Earth and Water, was used by the ancient Greeks to describe the characteristics of human behavior. These elements were applied in describing personalities by their "humours", sanguine, choleric, melancholic, and phlegmatic. Hippocrates (c.460-c.370 BC) included the four temperaments in his medical theories and practice. (For a complete history of temperament, see Dorian Giesler Greenbaum's excellent book *Temperament: Astrology's Forgotten Key* (2005). When I studied with Joan McEvers and Marion March, I learned to add up the planets in their signs to find the elements and modalities in order to determine temperament. In the study presented here, I have developed an astrological method to determine the temperamental type of a child based on modern child development concepts. I hope it can be helpful to other astrologers. My purpose from the beginning, as stated in the Preface, was to be able to understand the child on the deepest level.

Chapter 1

Temperament and Quality of Mood

"Everyone is kneaded out of the same dough but not baked in the same oven."

Yiddish Proverb

Temperament is the "how" of behavior. To illustrate, think of placing an infant in a crib to sleep. A few hours later, one infant will still be in the same exact spot; another infant will somehow have managed to move to the other end of the crib. There is an observable difference in their behavior. To illustrate further, envision a mother nursing her baby when someone walks into the room. One infant will stop sucking and turn his head to look at this person while another will stay engrossed in feeding and ignore the distraction. The difference in behavior of the two infants is due to differences in temperament.

Temperament is present at birth. I believe that when the newborn takes that first breath, the activated natal chart can reveal the nature of that temperament. Temperament is observable and measureable. That is the key. As Bruce Scofield has pointed out (2001), many psychological terms like "ego", "self", "personality", and "drive", have "fuzzy" definitions that are not universally accepted and are subject to change. Temperament has been used by astrologers for centuries but mostly as an added rather than a central factor. It has not been given the in-depth attention deserved. With temperament so prominent in the development of children, astrologers should consider its importance in analyzing a natal birth chart.

Zodiac signs can be divided into four elements, Fire, Air, Earth and Water, considered for millennia as the basis for all life. Modern Jungian concepts of ego functions (ways of perceiving and interpreting reality) easily relate to the elements: sensation (Earth); thinking (Air);

intuition (Fire); and feeling (Water). Elements can also be divided into two categories: male, active, positive, Yang (Fire and Air) or Female, passive, negative, Yin (Water and Earth).

Fire represents action for the purpose of initiating things, warmth, spirit, enthusiasm, creativity, courage.

Air represents the intellect, communication, learning and knowledge, sociability.

Earth represents stability and containment, the practical and materialistic, power and strength, structure.

Water represents emotions, compassion, imagination, nurturing, sensitivity.

An individual can be balanced in the elements or there may be an imbalance caused by too much of one element and too little of another, for instance. There are also compatible combinations and incompatible combinations.

The signs can also be divided into three modes of functioning: Cardinal, Fixed, and Mutable. These represent the elements' expression and style of behavior.

Cardinal is assertive, initiating, future-oriented and active with the power to lead.

Fixed is stable, self-contained, determined, persistent, resistant to change, based in the here and now.

Mutable is flexible, adaptable to new things, changeable, transitioning energy.

By combining the elements and modalities, we come to the root power of each sign. I call this the Astrological Type, to distinguish it from the Temperamental Type (such as the "shy" child) found in Child Development. An Astrological Type is thus defined as the combined element and modality, such as Cardinal/Fire or Fixed/Earth or Mutable/Air. The Cardinal/Fire person, for instance, could then be described as a warm, enthusiastic person who is an assertive, initiating leader. The Fixed/Earth person is one who, by his ability to sustain his efforts over a long period of time, is able to complete what the Cardinal/Fire person has started. The Mutable/Air person adds his ability to communicate possible adjustments needed to improve what's been done.

I use the elements and modalities of astrology to find the components of temperament. I do not use the houses of the chart; I view them as fields of experience the child will encounter in life. Temperament from birth on will be shaped and modified by environmental influences; it may be enhanced and heightened or it may be diminished and repressed. It is the two-way interaction between child and environment which continues as a dynamic process throughout childhood into adolescence and eventual adulthood. This developmental course requires a second book to explore it in depth.

I developed my own method for finding the Astrological Type in the natal chart. (For a blank Worksheet #1 see Appendix C). I have weighted each factor according to its importance, from the Sun and its ruler, the Moon, the Ascendant and its ruler, and then the planets. The points total one hundred. I fill in the blanks next to each factor with the signs, then the points for each element and modality. These also add to one hundred so you can check if you have added correctly. I can then determine the Astrological Type. Below I can note any lack or overemphasis of an element. I give points in each of the blanks found in the compatible and incompatible combinations because these will help illuminate other components. In the notes section I can analyze what I have found. My analysis of the elements is based largely on the energy approach to astrology developed by Stephen Arroyo in *Astrology, Psychology, and the Four Elements* (1975). I have created a numerical scale (see Appendix C) by which to categorize my findings as falling into the very high or low, average or normal, or extremes of high and low categories.

I've chosen the natal charts of a brother and sister, Hayden and Clara, to use throughout all of the chapters for illustrating the method of determining the temperamental components. They were chosen because I've known them since birth and have been able to

4   Kidwheels

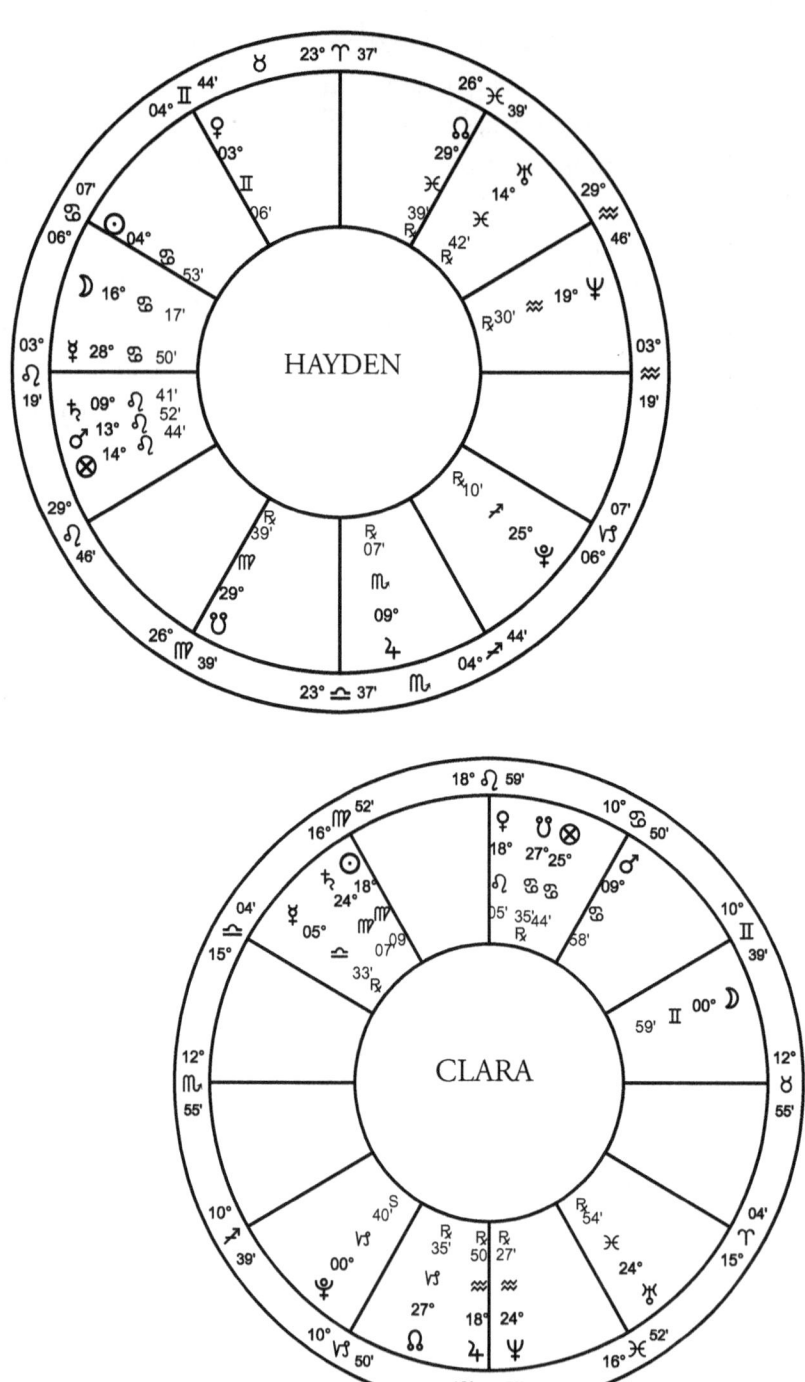

Worksheet #1: ASTROLOGICAL TYPE

NAME Hayden **DATA** Withheld for confidentiality

Fill in blanks with appropriate signs. Add up points for elements and qualities.

PLANET	SIGN	POINTS		ELEMENT TOTALS	
Sun	Can	20		Fire	19
Sun Ruler	Can	20		Earth	0
Moon	Can	15		Air	6
Ascendant	Leo	10		Water	75
Asc. Ruler	Can	10		Total	100
Mercury	Can	5			
Venus	Gem	5		QUALITY TOTALS	
Mars	Leo	5		Cardinal	70
Jupiter	Sco	4		Fixed	23
Saturn	Leo	3		Mutable	7
Uranus	Pisc	1		Total	100
Neptune	Aqu	1			
Pluto	Sag	1		ASTROLOGICAL TYPE	
Total		100		Cardinal/Water	

Lack of: Earth/Air   Over-emphasis on: Water

COMPATIBLE COMBINATIONS   **INCOMPATIBLE COMBINATIONS**
Water/Earth: 75   Air/Water: 81   Water/Fire: 94
Air/Fire: 25   Air/Earth: 6   Earth/Fire: 19

QUALITY OF MOOD
Check one according to levels of Fire/Air (over 65), balanced (35-65), Water/Earth (over 65)

Positive   Balanced   Negative *Yes*

watch them grow. I will also use other charts from my sample group as further examples.

From the completed worksheet above, we can see that Hayden is highest in the Water element, Fire next, little Air and no Earth. He is highest in the quality of Cardinality so his astrological type is Cardinal Water. There is an incompatible combination of Fire/Water at eighty-one points which indicates a conflict between his need for independence and a need for attachment.

Worksheet #1: ASTROLOGICAL TYPE

NAME Clara   **DATA** Withheld for confidentiality

Fill in blanks with appropriate signs. Add up points for elements and qualities.

PLANET	SIGN	POINTS	ELEMENT TOTALS	
Sun	Vir	20	Fire	5
Sun Ruler	Lib	20	Earth	34
Moon	Gem	15	Air	45
Ascendant	Sco	10	Water	16
Asc. Ruler	Cap	10	Total	100
Mercury	Lib	5		
Venus	Leo	5	QUALITY TOTALS	
Mars	Can	5	Cardinal	41
Jupiter	Aq	4	Fixed	20
Saturn	Vir	3	Mutable	39
Uranus	Pisc	1	Total	100
Neptune	Aq	1		
Pluto	Cap	1	ASTROLOGICAL TYPE	
Total		100	Cardinal/Air	

Lack of: Fire   Overemphasis on: None

COMPATIBLE COMBINATIONS   **INCOMPATIBLE COMBINATIONS**
Water/Earth: 50   Air/Water: 61   Water/Fire: 21
Air/Fire: 50   Air/Earth: 79   Earth/Fire: 39

QUALITY OF MOOD
Check one according to levels of Fire/Air (over 65), balanced (35-65), Water/Earth (over 65)

Positive   Balanced **50**   Negative

    In contrast, Clara's worksheet shows that she is highest in Air, then Earth, less in Water and little Fire. In the qualities, Cardinality is highest with Mutability right behind and less Fixed.

    The compatible combinations show that both combinations are balanced. In spite of her Virgo Sun, Clara is basically a Cardinal/Air type, although Mutable/Air is a close second. Air/Earth is the highest incompatible combination which could indicate more detachment and less emotionalism, but the fact that both Sun and Moon are ruled by Mercury in Libra helps ease the difficulties.

Quality of Mood

Some babies are born with a generally happy, easy-going, and positive nature. Mother breathes a sigh of relief, knowing that they have been blessed with an "easy" child. Maybe their first child was more difficult. If this is the first child, the mother often fools herself into thinking this happy baby is the result of her good parenting. But, oh, that second child!

This category of behavior describes the overall mood element of temperament: the amount of pleasant, friendly behavior as contrasted with unpleasant, crying, unfriendly behavior (Thomas, Chess & Birch, 1968). Some children are more balanced in outlook, responding appropriately to the given situation. When a child exhibits pleasant, friendly behavior, he/she is scored as positive mood. Crying, whining, unfriendly behavior is scored as negative mood. Those considered balanced are scored medium. Since elements of the signs in Fire and Air are rated positive (active) and elements in Earth and Water are rated negative (passive), it is easy to determine quality of mood based on these combinations. If the level of Fire/Air is over 65, the child is predominantly of positive mood. If the level of Earth/Water is over 65, the child's overall mood is negative. If both levels fall between 35-65, mood is balanced and appropriate to the situation. However, it should be noted that when the positive is higher than the negative, the child will tend to be more positive in mood than the child who is higher in negative mood. It is all a matter of degree. Rarely will there be a child who is 50/50, like Clara, and then other factors should be taken into account.

The incompatible combinations add subtle nuances to the overall mood, but only those with the highest numbers should be included in the analysis. These are based on the fact that some elements don't mix well and have different effects on the child's mood. Good descriptions of these imbalances can be found in Arroyo's book *Astrology,*

Psychology, and the Four Elements (1975) and in F*inding the Person in the Horoscope* by Zipporah Dobbins (1973). These nuances can add a lot to your analysis of variations in mood.

The child's overall mood should be noted on the worksheet. Hayden's worksheet shows a level of 75 in Earth/Water and only 25 in Fire/Air so his mood is more negative, though not extreme. Clara's worksheet shows a different picture with 50 in each category and, therefore, well balanced.

From all the data gathered from the chart and worksheet, I can now begin to analyze what I have learned about Hayden and Clara which I write in the Notes section.

About Hayden I wrote: "Hayden is very sensitive to experience. Timidity and fear cause negative reactions to anything new. He is likely to withdraw into his inner world because of his insecurities. As he grows older, these may develop into compassion for others with a desire to help them. He is not grounded in the physical world (lack of earth), he fears growing up, and has a conflict between his desire for independence and a need for attachment (emphasis on Fire/Water). He needs a strong structure in his daily routines to give him a sense of security. His fear of new ideas and people may cause him to become physical or act out if he is pushed too far. His overall mood falls in the high range on the negative side. He tends to appear serious most of the time."

About Clara, I wrote: "Clara's forte is expression in words. She operates from a rational approach to experience (emphasis on Air). She is very sociable. She does not have a strong connection to the emotions of others and may lack sensitivity, even seem cold and aloof at times. The feelings of others are not as important as her own. She is driven to put her ideas into concrete form (emphasis on Air/Earth). A lack of vitality (lack of Fire) may lead to a vulnerability to any type of infection such as frequent colds, even asthma."

These notes give me a contextual background for the temperamental components you'll learn about in the following chapters. To further illustrate the concept of mood, examine two more charts from my sample of children. Anthony has 85 points in Fire/Air. He came

Temperament and Quality of Mood 9

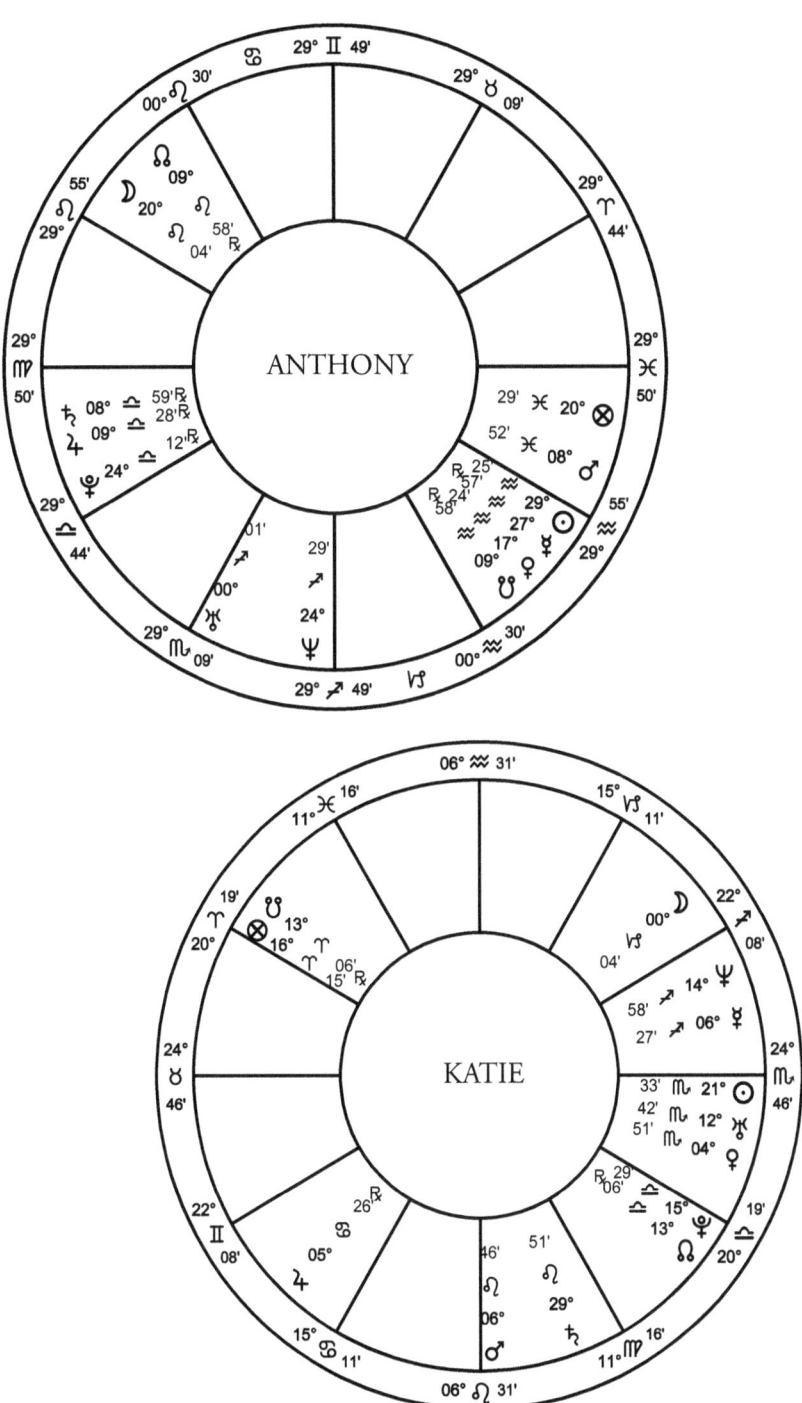

to school eager to learn. He had a great ability to express himself in every way. He was smiling and friendly with a great deal to say about everything. He made friends quickly and easily because of his perpetual positive mood. His wonderful sense of humor was evident at an early age. His warm, friendly attitude also elicited warm friendly responses from teachers as well as children.

Katie was one of a set of identical twins born four minutes apart. Her chart and worksheet show a high level of Earth/Water combination. She and her sister entered school at age two with a very negative mood and cried continually for weeks. Strongly placed in Fixed signs, it took a long time before they adapted to the school environment. Throughout their time at the Center, they whined a lot and generally demonstrated a sullen, negative attitude. Those children with a negative mood usually elicit annoyed responses from adults.

The next chapter will examine the components of approach/withdrawal and adaptability.

Chapter 2

Approach/Withdrawal and Adaptability

Approach/Withdrawal

"Don't underestimate me because I'm quiet. I know more than I speak and observe more than you know."

Kyla Lanier

One infant spits out a new food that's presented to him while another accepts it easily. Curiosity and eagerness to explore propels one child into his new preschool. Another child clings to her mother's legs. This ability to approach something new versus withdrawing from it is the temperamental trait termed approach/withdrawal. It describes the child's initial and usual response to anything new; foods, places, people or situations. A child with positive emotionality shows interest, an eagerness to explore and investigate. There is a positive anticipation demonstrated by smiling, laughing and motor activity such as clapping hands. Alternatively, a child with negative emotionality meets anything new with a definite "no" by avoiding contact, appearing tense, crying and trying to get away.

Jerome Kagan, an eminent psychologist, has been studying this one component of temperament for over 20 years at Harvard University (2004). He conducted two longitudinal studies covering infants of 4 months to their adolescence. Those children who reacted negatively to anything unfamiliar with frequent motor activity (thrashing of legs, arching the back and crying) he termed "high-reactive" or "inhibited". Those that reacted more positively were called "low-reactive" or "uninhibited". These behavioral tendencies were grouped by the following descriptions:

High-reactives tend to be introverted, cautious, dependent for emotional support on family, and to avoid unfamiliar people, objects and events.

Low-reactives tend to be extroverted, competitive, bolder, sociable and confident.

Kagan's research was also duplicated elsewhere with social animals such as dogs, baboons, and monkeys.

Before getting into withdrawal in children, it's important to note that all children go through a period of "stranger anxiety" which appears around six months in the form of wary reactions to strangers. This phase continues to escalate through the first birthday. Anxiety is lessened if the child is at home, in mother's arms and if the adult is smiling and friendly. Stranger anxiety would be more intense in "shy" and "difficult" child temperamental types. Stranger anxiety is not the same as initial approach/withdrawal in a child's temperament.

The key for automatic responses to the environment is the Ascendant. In *Astrology, Karma and Transformation* (1978) Arroyo talks about the connection between the Ascendant and the physical body (p.214) and whether or not there is conductivity or resistance to the energy flowing directly to the body. There are many levels of meaning given to the Ascendant, of course. In this instance, the Ascendant becomes the key to determining the child's initial response to anything new or unfamiliar. Additional points include aspects of planets to the Ascendant that energize or inhibit the flow of energy: Jupiter and Saturn. Jupiter expands while Saturn restricts. An additional factor is the Ascendant ruler whose importance lies in its distinction as the chart ruler. The overall mood of the child adds to the picture. For instance, temperamentally shy or difficult children have negative moods and withdraw from anything unfamiliar. Positive mood children are more apt to approach new things eagerly.

The signature for either approach or withdrawal can be seen in Worksheet #2 which is based on the scores in Worksheet #1 (blank version in Appendix C). By applying this to Hayden's chart we see:

Approach/Withdrawal and Adaptability

	Approach		**Withdrawal**	
30	Positive Mood	0	Negative Mood	30
25	Fire or Air Asc.	25	Earth or Water Asc.	0
20	Fire or Air Asc. ruler	0	Water or Earth Asc. ruler	20
15	Jupiter conj. Asc.	0	Saturn conj. Asc.	15
10	Jupiter aspects to Asc.	10	Saturn aspects to Asc.	0
	Total	**35**	**Total**	**65**

In Hayden's chart, his approach number is on the low side while his withdrawal number falls on the high side. Both fall at the extremes of the normal range. Anything new or unfamiliar to Hayden was met with withdrawal and resistance. His initial response to his first Easter egg hunt, for instance, was fear, crying and refusal to participate. Entering kindergarten the first time produced crying and vomiting. There has been a lot of dependence on the parents for emotional support but things have improved over the years.

Clara's mood is well balanced. I gave her points for positive mood because she is high in Air on Worksheet #1.

Worksheet #2: ADAPTABILITY/WITHDRAWAL

Name: Clara

	Approach		**Withdrawal**	
30	Positive Mood	30	Negative Mood	0
25	Fire or Air Asc.	0	Earth or Water Asc.	30
20	Fire or Air Asc. ruler	0	Water or Earth Asc. ruler	20
15	Jupiter conj. Asc.	0	Saturn conj. Asc.	0
10	Jupiter aspects to Asc.	10	Saturn aspects to Asc.	0
	Total	**40**	**Total**	**50**

Both numbers for approach/withdrawal in Clara's chart show her to be well balanced. Her approach or withdrawal from new things will vary with the situation. She may withdraw from some things initially, but she will adapt very quickly.

Adaptability

"It is not the strongest or the most intelligent who will survive but those who can best manage change."

Charles Darwin

Closely related to approach/withdrawal is adaptability. After the initial response to something new, how easily or quickly does the child adapt to the new situation? Watching children enter the preschool for the first time, I found many variations in their responses. Some children adjusted in a day or two. Some took weeks, even months to feel comfortable in the classroom. One two-year old fell to the floor kicking and screaming so loudly other adults came to see what we were doing to the poor child. Another little girl wrapped her arms and legs around her mother and had to be peeled from her every morning for weeks. A third girl accepted being in school but did not participate in any activities for a month. She preferred to sit and watch the other children play. Gradually, she became involved in the activities. One quiet child would stand in the doorway for 20 minutes watching the children before she became engaged. No amount of encouragement or coaxing her to join in worked. We learned it was best to just say 'Good morning' and allow her time to adapt.

We were always glad to see a child enter the classroom eagerly, ready to jump into the activities. There might be a question or two as to when Mommy would return but that was easier to contend with than the many crying children needing attention.

In the birth charts, there was a predominance of Air and mutability that predicted the level of adaptability. I created Worksheet #3 to determine the level of adaptability in a child's chart. It is based on scores from Worksheet #1 and points are given only to the elements and qualities that have 25 points or more. Examining Hayden's chart shows little Air or mutability. His overall score for adaptability is 30 which puts him in the low category. It takes some time and encouragement from his parents before he eventually adapts; coupled with his overall negative mood and tendency to withdraw from new things, he tends to have difficulty facing new experiences and takes some time before he adapts to them. He should not be coaxed or pushed but allowed time to get used to something new.

Worksheet #3: ADAPTABILITY

Name: Hayden

Points	Elements & Qualities	
30	Mutability (25+)	0
20	Cardinality (25+)	20
15	Air (25+)	0
15	Fire (25+)	0
10	Water (25+)	10
10	Earth (25+)	0
	Total	**30**

Notes: (Examine the total in terms of Low (0-35), Balanced (35-65) or High (65-100).

His sister, Clara, adapts very quickly. Her score is in the high range with 75 points. She entered school with little fuss and adapted quickly.

Worksheet #3: ADAPTABILITY

Name: Clara

Points	Elements & Qualities	
30	Mutability (25+)	30
20	Cardinality (25+)	20
15	Air (25+)	15
15	Fire (25+)	0
10	Water (25+)	0
10	Earth (25+)	10
	Total	**75**

16 Kidwheels

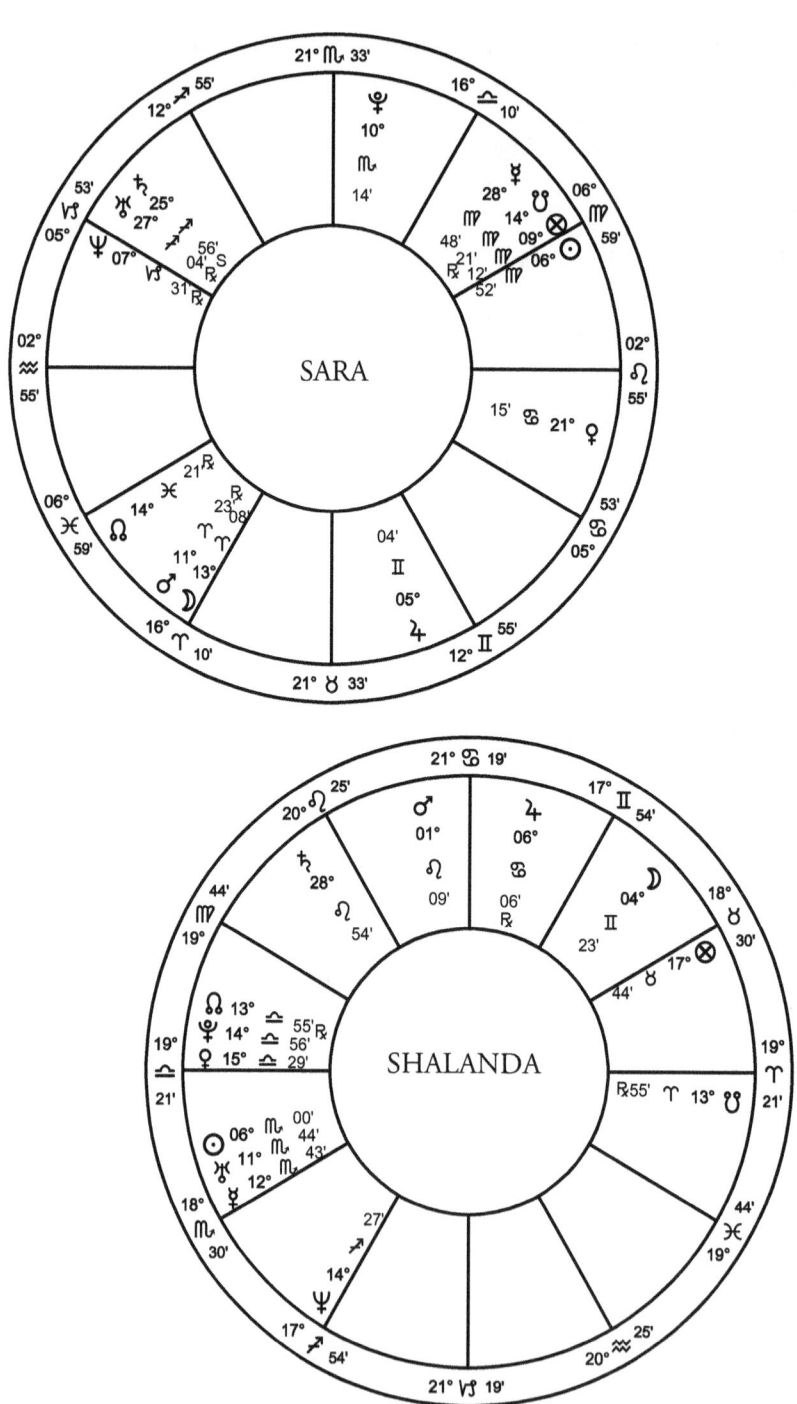

Sara's chart is another example of a child with a positive approach who is easily adaptable. The elements are well balanced with Water/Earth having the edge. The close trine of Jupiter to the Ascendant gives her a positive approach to new experiences. She will take a minute to size things up and then dive in with enthusiasm. For example, she was cautious on the first trip on her parent's boat but quickly came to enjoy it immensely.

Shalanda's chart is an example of a child who entered school with a very positive approach and adapted quickly. Although she has three planets in Scorpio in the first House, including her Sun, she is a Cardinal Air type. She was extremely verbal at a young age and insistent on expressing her opinions on everything. She was very pretty, sociable and well-liked by other children. Her strong independence and confidence in herself made her a natural leader.

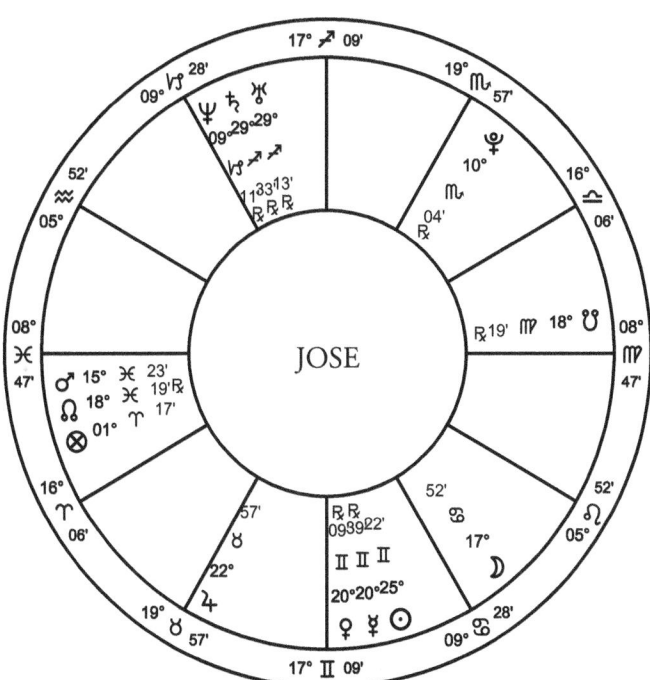

Jose is an example of a boy with a positive mood but with a higher withdrawal than approach to new things (although both are in the normal range). His reactions tended to be intense but mostly on the positive side. He was not happy entering school for the first time but his adaptability level is so high (70 points) as well as a high distractibility level (80 points) that he adjusted very quickly. Being very verbal, he was able to express his needs. With the Grand Water trine, the Mars in Pisces in trine to the Moon in Cancer, he was very sweet and rarely got into conflict with other children. He also delighted others with his sense of humor.

Since the research indicates that 40 percent of children fall into the "easy child" category, most charts of children you will see will have a positive approach and rapid adaptability. The "slow-to-warm-up" children who demonstrate an initial withdrawal to new things and slow adaptability number about 15-20 percent.

Chapter 3

Intensity of Reaction and Threshold of Response

Intensity of Reaction

> *"Intensity is so much more becoming in the young."*
> Joanne Woodward

Among children you will find the screamers and the whiners, the ones who smile and the ones who laugh explosively; ones that tantrum when told "no" and ones that just pout; ones that cry the hardest and those that whimper. The temperament component which defines these behaviors is called intensity of reaction. It describes the child's response to either internal states such as hunger or pain or to external stimuli such as new foods, dressing, bathing, attempts by parents to control. The focus is on the energy output of the response irrespective of its direction being either positive or negative. It is usually the extremes which are a source of problems. Children with strong responses tend to provoke equally strong responses from others. "Don't be so dramatic!" complains a mother to her screaming child. Loud responses of children can be a source of embarrassment to parents, particularly in public places. Another problem comes from caretakers so used to over-reactions they ignore a child who may be seriously hurt. Intense children draw attention to themselves, and that attention is usually negative. Children with mild reactions are more easily managed but can just as easily be overlooked because they are not demanding. Because of their quiet demeanor, it is often difficult to judge how they feel. Their responses can even be misinterpreted. For example, a child may not get excited over a gift or a pony ride which is thought of as being ungrateful. It is really because the child has difficulty expressing pleasure in an intense manner. The following comparisons may be helpful:

Intensity of Reaction

To:	Intense Response	Mild response
Hunger	Cries, screams	Whimpers
New Foods	Spits it out, cries	Holds in mouth, drools
Dressing	Screams if restrained	Cooperates with little fuss
Toy taken away	Cries, fights	Gives in, plays with something else
Being full	Knocks away cup or spoon	Turns head away
Being told "no"	Screams, tantrums	Gives in, pouts
Pleasure	Loud laughter, claps hands	Smiles, chuckles

Charts of children observed with high, intense reactions had similar elements such as Moon aspects to Mars, both aspected to the Ascendant, Moon in Aries or in the 1st house as well as a Jupiter aspect to the Moon, Mars or the Ascendant. The less intense children lacked these signatures. They also tended to have Fixed or Earth Moons. See Worksheet #4 below.

To measure intensity of reaction, I assigned points to each part of the configuration as follows:

Worksheet #4: Intensity of Reaction

NAME   DATA

Examine the chart and assign points as follows:

Points	Aspects	
30	Moon aspects to Mars	_____
20	Mars aspects to Asc.	_____
20	Moon aspects to Asc.	_____
15	Moon in Aries	_____
10	Moon in 1st house	_____
5	Jupiter aspects to Moon, Mars or Asc.	_____
100	**Total**	_____

Notes: Points between 35 to 65 indicate average intensity, 20-35 indicate low intensity, 5-20 extremely low, 65-80 high, 80-95 extremely high. Most children will fall into the average category. Few children fall in the extreme category.

However, nothing in astrology is ever that simple. There are always a few exceptions to the rule which require deeper study for an explanation. Some children with the intensity signature in their charts did not always behave as expected. The reason, I discovered, lay in the study of incompatible combinations of the elements. Here I must thank Zipporah Dobyns (*Finding the Person in the Horoscope*, 1973) and Stephen Arroyo (*Astrology, Psychology, and the Four Elements*, 1975) for descriptions of these combinations. Fire and Air are considered "expressive" while Earth and Water are "repressive". Various combinations produce different ways that children express their feelings. The compatible combinations of Fire/Air and Earth/Water, as shown in Chapter One, indicate the child's overall mood as positive or negative. A study of the incompatible combinations adds to the picture of the child's intensity of reaction, like variations on a theme. For instance, Water dampens Fire, Water and Earth create mud, Fire and Earth produce fiery lava, Air and Water create fog or mist.

Worksheet #4: Intensity of Reaction

Name: Hayden

Points	Aspects	
30	Moon aspects to Mars	30
20	Mars aspects to Asc.	0
20	Moon aspects to Asc.	0
15	Moon in Aries	0
10	Moon in 1st house	0
5	Jupiter aspects to Moon, Mars or Asc.	5
100		**Total** 35

We return to the charts of Hayden and Clara as examples of how this works. (See Chapter 1 for charts.) Hayden's intensity of reaction score is 35 which puts him at the lowest point of the average scale. In the element combinations he is high in Air/Water (81) and even more in Water/Fire (94). (See his Worksheet #1) His Air/Water combination makes him somewhat of a dreamer who lives a lot in his head. The Fire/Water category is a little tricky because it has two faces: the first is the individual with mood swings, from depression to emotional outbursts, as well as a conflict between the need for independence and attachment; the second is the person who is a warm, caring individual. Hayden is serious and negative in overall mood but his emotional reactions are generally mild and warm until he is pushed too far by his parents. Then he is likely to explode in anger.

Worksheet #4: Intensity of Reaction

Name: Clara

Points	Aspects	
30	Moon aspects to Mars	0
20	Mars aspects to Asc.	20
20	Moon aspects to Asc.	0
15	Moon in Aries	0
10	Moon in 1st house	0
5	Jupiter aspects to Moon, Mars or Asc.	5
100	**Total**	25

Clara's intensity signature falls in the low category of 25 points. Her element combinations show an emphasis on Air/Earth (79) with Air/Water (61) as second. Her overall mood is balanced with an edge to the positive because she is strongest in the Air element. The Air/Earth type shows little emotion. Clara is more practical and logical in her approach to things compared to Hayden. She, too, is high in the Air/Water combination and has a lively imagination. Her Virgo Sun and Gemini Moon are ruled by the planet Mercury in Libra which is the focal point of a T-square. She does not show much emotion unless she is thwarted in some way (Mars opposing Pluto as the other part of the T-square) and then she expresses extreme anger.

Samuel's chart is a good example of a child with high intensity. His overall mood is positive with 72 percent Fire/Air. Though his Sun is in Taurus, he is a Mutable Air type. He has a positive approach to anything new and is very adaptable. His intensity range is high (70 points). The most predominant combination of elements is Air/Earth which makes him more detached and goal oriented. There is also a lack of Water (the feeling element) in his chart. Samuel is able to express what he is feeling through words. He gets uncomfortable around people who are highly emotional. Because of his highly positive mood, his intensity comes across as a great enthusiasm for life. His distinct laughter can be heard across a wide expanse.

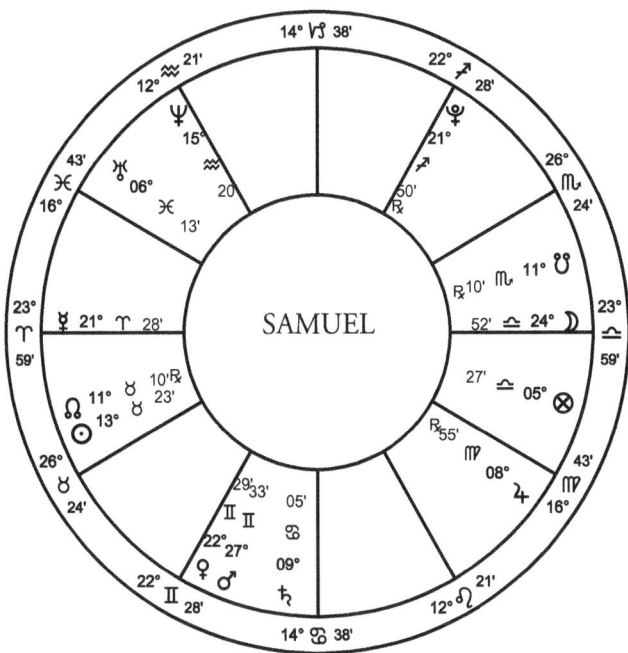

Donny's chart is an example of one that is contradictory. His intensity figure is high (70) but it was not immediately noticeable when he entered preschool. He seemed a quiet, dependent child who showed little emotion. However, when aroused by conflict with a teacher or another child, his reaction was intense and often violent. He could be disruptive, impulsive, and often acted sadistically toward other children. Donny was predominately Air/Earth (85) which accounts for his lack of emotion. He also lacked Fire and Water. Two things in the chart which repressed the intensity of his reactions were both Moon and Mars in Earth. The violence he displayed arose from the Moon, Mars and Venus being involved in a T-square with Saturn and Uranus. Another problem arises from having two stellia: Moon, Venus, Mars in Taurus ruled by Venus; and Sun, Jupiter and Mercury in Gemini ruled by Mercury. There is little connection between the two stellia, which can give rise to psychological problems. Donny could verbalize the rules of behavior but rarely followed them. Socially, he did not form close attachments to anyone. Everything the staff attempted failed to bring about a change in his behavior, and suggestions to the mother to seek counseling resulted in his being withdrawn from school.

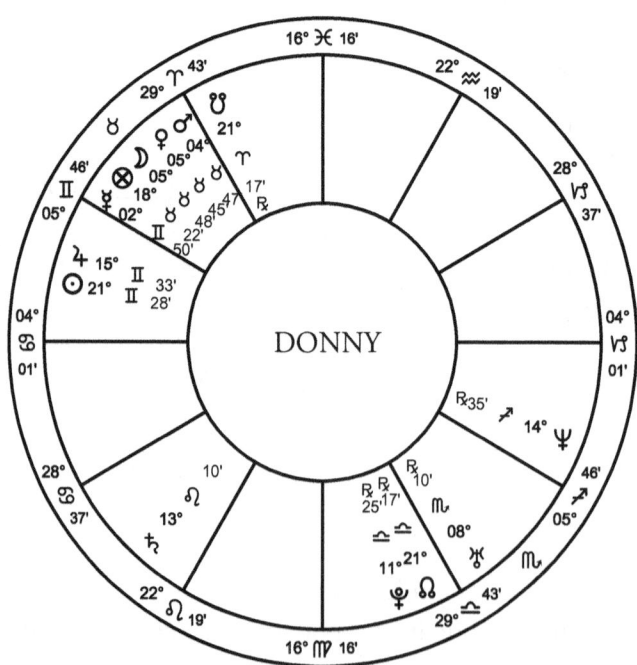

Intensity of Reaction and Threshold of Response

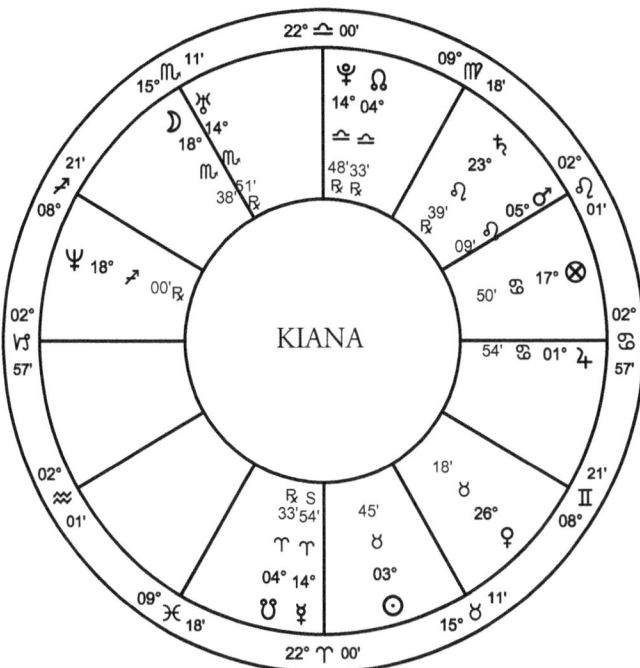

Kiana's intensity of reaction is low (25) and she has a fixed Moon. Her chart shows a high level of Earth and Fire. This combination shows her ability to control and direct the energy of Fire into hard work and achieving her goals.

Sara is another example of high intensity (70). (See her chart in Chapter 2.) The Moon/Mars conjunction in Aries was obvious, even as an infant. When hungry, she would work herself up into a red-faced, screaming tantrum. The tantrums continued throughout her childhood which was frequently embarrassing for her mother. The Moon/Mars conjunction is also inconjunct Pluto which added endurance to the tantrums. Once she got started, it was difficult for her to stop. Fortunately, she is also heavily Fire and Earth which eventually enabled her to direct all that energy into a successful career as an interior designer. At age 22, she still has a temper but now has learned how to control it when she needs to.

Threshold of Response

> *"We are the children of our landscape; it dictates behavior and even thought in the measure to which we are responsive to it."*
>
> Lawrence Durrell

Closely related to intensity action is the Threshold of Response. What level of a sensory stimulation (sight, sound, taste, smell, touch, pain) is required for the child to respond? Some children are very sensitive to certain fabrics, textures of foods, changes to sound, or bright lights. The less sensitive child is not as particular about these things and is less likely to put up a fuss.

"He wakes at the slightest sound," says one mother.

"She can sleep through anything," says another.

"Once Samuel finds a pair of pants he's comfortable wearing, it's difficult to get him to wear anything else."

"My daughter jumps at any loud noise."

To find the threshold of response in children's charts, I turned to a technique I learned about in the classes of Marion March and Joan McEvers called "Tempo of Adjustment". This technique was elaborated on by Marc Edmond Jones (*Essentials of Astrological Analysis,* 1960) and later in *The Mountain Astrologer* (Aug/Sept, 2001) by Bob Makransky (p.73). "Mental chemistry," as it was called, is determined by two factors: the speed of the Moon and whether Mercury precedes or trails the Sun in the chart. They were referring to the perceptual capabilities of the Moon. When the Moon is fast (the mean being 13 degrees, 10 minutes), the individual is alert. When the Moon is slow, the individual is more deliberate. The child with the fast Moon takes in a broad arena of sensory information. The slow Moon child is more focused on what is most interesting, excluding that which is less interesting.

When Mercury, which indicates the response to what is perceived, is preceding the Sun, the child is eager, while the child with Mercury trailing the Sun is certain. Mercury is the conscious awareness of the situation and the rational means by which the individual interprets and responds. The eager type is quick to jump in (and often jumps to conclusions). The certain type is more cautious in reacting to things. Imagine a teacher asking a question to her class. Some children will immediately be waving their hands in the air for recognition. Other children take longer to think about it before they respond. A good teacher will allow enough time to pass so that both types of children will have an opportunity to respond. Combining these two factors gives four possible types:

Type 1: Fast Moon, Mercury trailing the Sun. Alert/Certain type.

Type 2: Slow Moon, Mercury preceding the Sun. Eager/Deliberate type.

Type 3: Fast Moon, Mercury preceding the Sun. Alert/Eager type.

Type 4: Slow Moon, Mercury trails the Sun. Deliberate/Certain type.

In studying a child's chart, Types 1 and 2 would be considered "normal" or "average". Both perceptual and rational capabilities are balanced. Type 1 is quick to react but is not impulsive. Type 2 is more deliberate in perception but adaptable to the situation in response. They are more in tune with the pace of life around them and flexible enough to adapt to changing situations. Types 3 and 4 have more difficulty: Type 3 moves too fast and often has to backtrack to make adjustments while Type 4 moves too slow, becoming withdrawn and having to catch up or remaining stubbornly stuck where he is. Types 1 and 2 require less attention when analyzing the child's chart. Types 3 and 4 need further analysis because of their importance when combined with other elements in the temperament. In my sample of children, the various types were rather evenly distributed with 31 Type 1, 29 Type 2, 21 Type 3, and 30 Type 4. There were only 3 that I called "neutral" since the speed of the Moon fell at the mean and Mercury was conjunct the Sun. Sixty children fell into the "normal" group while 51 fell into the group with possible difficulties.

The Type 3 child is characterized by Marc Edmond Jones (1960) as having "……an altogether unnecessary impatience" (p.383). He acts by impulse and instinct, is more experimental while less concerned with consequences. The tendency is to move before he thinks, therefore mistakes are frequently made, forcing him to return to make corrections. Because he follows his immediate inclinations, he is less concerned about what anyone else may think about it. He likes to jump right into situations and his general optimism allows him to bounce right back when things get difficult. He is also more likely to notice subtle changes in his environment.

The Type 4 child moves slowly with caution. They don't jump in like their counterparts but prefer to hang back and scope things out. She reacts based on past experience and is more subject to social authority. She is slow to react. She is more focused on what she wants or what she is afraid of rather than spending time processing any peripheral sensory data. She has to be more sure of herself before she acts. For this reason, she is more oriented toward achieving her goals. She has difficulty in situations requiring quick decisions. She is more likely to stick to her old ways in a stubborn manner rather than to look forward and try new ways.

Hayden is a Type 4 with his slow Moon and Mercury trailing the Sun. The fact that he is deliberate, approaching anything new with caution, is reinforced by his tendency for withdrawal as his initial response (Worksheet #2). Hayden requires more time for deliberation before he acts. He focuses well on any project until it is accomplished so he does well in school. He may not get the attention some of his quicker classmates get, but he gets recognition for his ability to get things done.

Clara is better balanced as a Type 1 with a fast Moon and Mercury trailing the Sun. She is eager and responsive but is not impulsive. She follows where her particular interest leads her but then can concentrate on what needs to be done to accomplish what she wants.

Samuel is Type 3, the alert eager child who is impatient and impulsive. He is one of those students instantly waving his hand in the air to answer the teacher's question. His clothes have to fit "just right" to feel comfortable. He hates loud noises and "icky" food. Because his perceptions are alert, he is quick to notice any changes in the environment.

Jean's chart is an example of a Type 2 child with a slow Moon and Mercury preceding the Sun. Jean has a positive approach to anything new and a low intensity of reaction. Elements are greatest in Fire/Earth, the "steam-roller" personality. Being a Type 2 enhances the Earth/Fire by being able to focus in on what she wants yet quick to evaluate the situation and decide on an action. Jean has become a lawyer, a profession that fits her Fire/Earth, Type 2 personality.

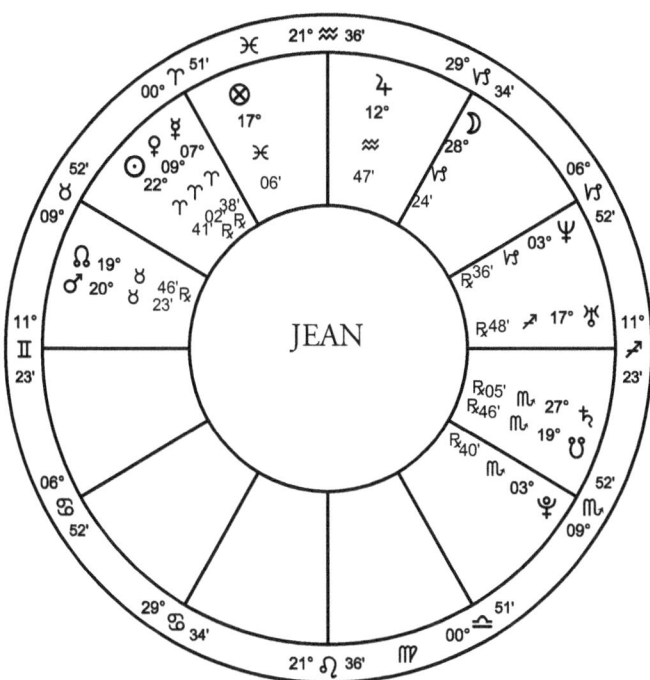

Chapter 4

Distractibility and Persistence

Distractibility and persistence are closely related because they are both concerned with attention span, the amount of time an individual can concentrate on or remain interested in something. Distractibility refers to how easily the child can be diverted from an ongoing activity. Persistence is how long a child will keep at an activity without giving up. Most children will be balanced in these two components; it is usually the children in the high or extreme category who run the risk of developing behavioral problems. It's important to study the two components together to see which predominates when they are out of balance.

Distractibility

"We say children are bad at paying attention, but we really mean that they're bad at not paying attention — they easily get distracted by anything interesting."

Alison Gopnik

Distractibility is a measure of how easily a child's ongoing behavior can be interrupted by another stimulus. For example, an infant may stop nursing if he hears a noise; a preschooler may lose interest in a story when the child next to her is talking; a school child will forget homework assignments. "Can't you remember anything?" demands an irritated mother, who can recognize the highly distractible child by the large number of jackets, keys, lunch boxes and other assorted items he's lost.

Distractibility is prized in infancy and toddler time when the child can easily be diverted from dangerous or annoying activities. Is the crawler showing too much interest in an electrical outlet? Just wave a colorful toy and his attention is instantly diverted. This quality, so welcome in the early years, becomes a problem when the child enters school. Now he is falling behind because of missing assignments. He is more interested in conversing with classmates than paying attention to the teacher. Mother can follow his trail through the house by the number of items he's dropped on the way to his room. On the positive side, the distractible child is tuned into her environment, has an alertness to nuances of behavior in people, and is more responsive in social situations. She is usually cheerful, outgoing and well-liked by others. And does she love to talk! Much to the teacher's chagrin! "Motor-mouth" is often the adjective used.

In a competitive environment such as school, distractibility is seen as a handicap which becomes equated with failure. Parents who stress the importance of achievement and high grades may respond in a harsh and punitive manner toward the child. They just don't understand it and really believe the child can "straighten up" if he wants to. The worst case scenario happens when parents or teachers decide the child has an attention-deficit disorder and search for a cure with medications. These disorders require a medical diagnosis and careful consideration as to whether or not this is a real disorder rather than an element of the child's temperament.

The level of distractibility in the child's chart can be determined by an examination of mutability, Air or Fire predominance, aspects to Mercury by Jupiter, Mars and Jupiter, Mercury conjunct the Ascendant, and Mercury in the signs of Gemini, Aries, Sagittarius and Pisces. The signature is weighted as follows (See full Worksheet #5 in Appendix C):

Points	Factors	
30	Mutability Predominance (from Worksheet #1)	____
25	Air/Fire Predominance (from Worksheet #1)	____
20	Mercury conjunct the Ascendant	____
15	Mercury aspects to Jupiter, Mars, Neptune	____
10	Mercury in Gemini, Sagittarius, Aries, Pisces, Virgo	____
	Total	____

Looking at Hayden's chart, we find this works out as:

Points	Factors	
30	Mutability Predominance (from Worksheet #1)	0
25	Air/Fire Predominance (from Worksheet #1)	0
20	Mercury conjunct the Ascendant	20
15	Mercury aspects to Jupiter, Mars, Neptune	0
10	Mercury in Gemini, Sagittarius, Aries, Pisces, Virgo	0
	Total	**20**

Hayden is very low on distractibility. He has a long attention span and can focus on a project until completed. This factor further emphasizes his Type 4 status in response level. He can work efficiently on the computer no matter what is going on around him. He spends many hours alone in his room working on complex Lego projects.

Clara's level of distractibility is higher than Hayden:

Points	Factors	
30	Mutability Predominance (from Worksheet #1)	30
25	Air/Fire Predominance (from Worksheet #1)	25
20	Mercury conjunct the Ascendant	0
15	Mercury aspects to Jupiter, Mars, Neptune	15
10	Mercury in Gemini, Sagittarius, Aries, Pisces, Virgo	0
	Total	**70**

She is more aware of changes in the environment than Hayden. Her attention span is shorter. She is also more outgoing and sociable. Her persistence level (next section) is high enough that no matter how often she is distracted, she will eventually return to complete her task.

For an illustration of a highly distractible child, examine David's chart. David came into preschool with a warm friendly attitude and adapted immediately without fuss. His preferred activity was to engage with other boys in construction with blocks or play with cars.

Distractibility and Persistence

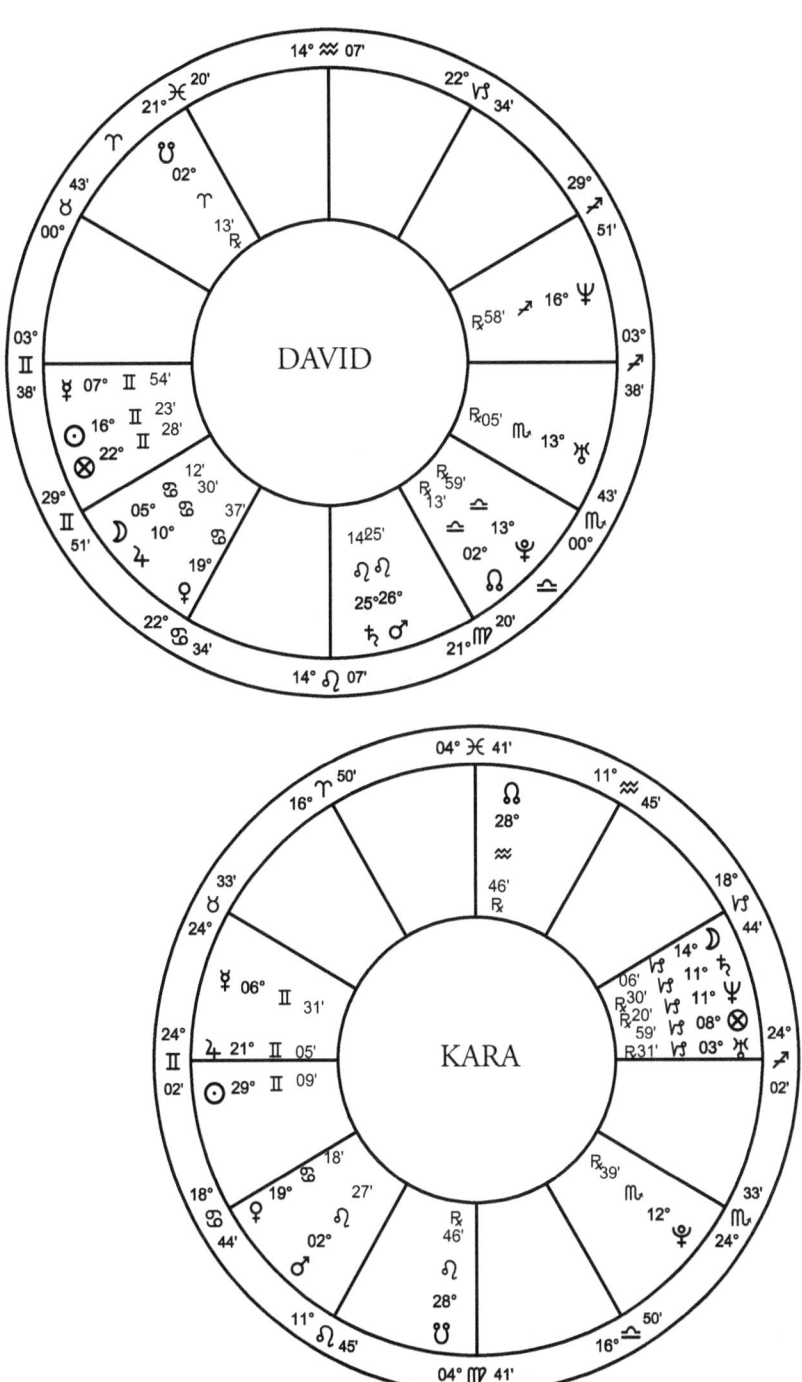

Observations of his behavior showed that he rarely completed tasks in other areas. Any activity that required continued, quiet attention, such as completing a puzzle, caused him to lose interest quickly to move on to something else. His distractibility level is very high (80 points). Such a high level will cause problems for him when he enters school where he will be expected to pay attention and complete assignments.

The next chart is Kara, the second daughter of another teacher from my school. The first daughter had no problems. Mother was aggravated with Kara who couldn't seem to keep track of her belongings or finish homework. It was driving the mother "crazy" because she had to constantly nag Kara to complete anything. Kara's distractibility level was extremely high (85 points). It was developing into a problem because of mother's high expectations for Kara's school performance. With a few suggestions on how to help Kara by changing her parenting practices, the situation gradually improved. Highly distractible children study better in a quiet room with fewer distractions. In addition, study should occur in short intervals with frequent breaks. Checklists are excellent tools for these children to keep track of their belongings, of things they need before leaving for school, and before leaving school for home. With patience and the appropriate techniques, the child can learn to function in ways that help them succeed.

Persistence

"It's not that I'm so smart, it's just that I stay with problems longer."
                                                                    Albert Einstein

Some children become so engrossed in an activity it's difficult to get them to transition to something new. Mother, ready for a trip to the store, finds her son building a tower of blocks. He refuses her request to stop with a loud "no". The more she insists, the more he resists until both are angry. Once in the store, the boy is attracted to a bag of sweets he wants. "No, it's too close to dinner," from mother sends him into a course of pleading, begging and nagging until she either gives in or drags him protesting out of the store. This scenario describes the persistent child whose attention span can focus on a task for a long time.

The persistent child may be difficult in the early years, but her ability to stay focused, pay attention and complete assignments is well rewarded when she enters school. Persistence equals accomplishment. Too much of a good thing, however, can evolve into a problem. Strong persistence can produce power struggles with others, particularly adults.

"That child is so stubborn!"

"When she wants something, she just keeps nagging until she gets it!"

When this behavior is met with parental anger and impatience, an oppositional conduct disorder can develop which needs outside assistance to resolve.

Persistence may not be equal in all activities. It can be found in gross motor activities where it can lead to athletic ability. It can also be seen in fine motor perceptual tasks such as Hayden's skill in constructing complex Lego projects. Insisting on having one's way creates problems in social relations. High persistence can also create problems when tied to other temperamental components such as high intensity level or high activity level. Whether parents perceive persistence as positive or negative depends on how much they value it in the child. Persistence in the chart is measured as follows:

Points	Factors	
30	Fixity Predominance (from Worksheet #1)	____
25	Earth/Water Predominance (from worksheet #1)	____
20	Mercury aspects to Saturn, Uranus, Pluto	____
15	Mars aspects to Saturn, Uranus, Pluto	____
10	Mercury in Taurus, Cancer, Leo, Libra, Scorpio, Capricorn or Aquarius	____
	Total	____

In examining a chart, persistence and distractibility should be evaluated together. For instance, a child with high distractibility and low persistence will have a lot more problems in school than another highly distractible child that has enough persistence to return to finish things. The child with high persistence and little distractibility is more likely to develop problems, particularly if the parents are punitive.

Hayden's persistence level is 70 points which puts him at the high end of the normal range. With his low distractibility level of 20 points, he does very well in school, is a good reader, and is able to focus well on any task without getting distracted.

Points	Factors	
30	Fixity Predominance (from Worksheet #1)	0
25	Earth/Water Predominance (from worksheet #1)	25
20	Mercury aspects to Saturn, Uranus, Pluto	20
15	Mars aspects to Saturn, Uranus, Pluto	15
10	Mercury in Taurus, Cancer, Leo, Libra, Scorpio, Capricorn or Aquarius	10
	Total	**70**

Clara has 60 points in persistence level. At the same time, her distractibility level is high (70 points) and she can easily be distracted by something more interesting but will eventually return to complete any activities left behind. What adds a level of persistence to Clara's chart is the T-square involving Mars, Mercury and Pluto. She becomes very willful, particularly when it comes to decision-making. She often throws temper tantrums when she doesn't get her way. Her piercing screams can be heard all through the house. In public places, her behavior results in immediate removal by parents so she can calm down. When faced with deciding between two things she considers equally desirable, she gets very agitated. Her father solved this problem to some extent by placing time constraints on her before taking over. Of course, this doesn't always work. She is like a Jekyll and Hyde personality—a sweet, smiling child one minute, a shrieking witch the next. Hayden has difficulty understanding her. "Dad, why does she act like that?" he frequently asks. Fortunately, most of her acting out occurs at home. Here's the persistence section of her worksheet:

Points	Factors	
30	Fixity Predominance (from Worksheet #1)	0
25	Earth/Water Predominance (from worksheet #1)	25
20	Mercury aspects to Saturn, Uranus, Pluto	20
15	Mars aspects to Saturn, Uranus, Pluto	15
10	Mercury in Taurus, Cancer, Leo, Libra, Scorpio, Capricorn or Aquarius	0
	Total	**60**

To look at more samples of the persistent child, we'll start with Ashley. Ashley presented a negative mood but did not withdraw from new things. She also adapted quickly. Her intensity of reaction was normal on the low side. Her persistence level was high (70 points). In the area of social relations, Ashley was intent on having her own way. She defied any adult who attempted to exert authority over her. Her Mars opposes the Ascendant, squares Mercury and is inconjunct to

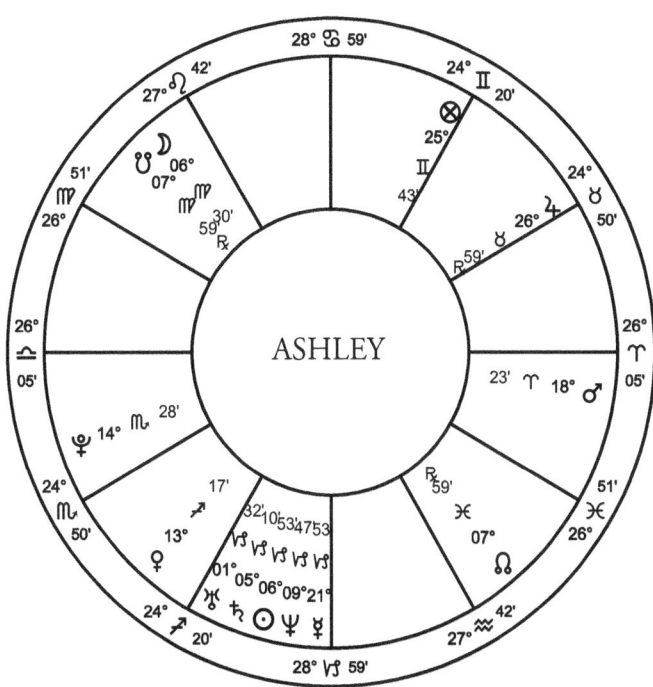

Pluto in the 1st house. She wasn't so much unhappy at being left in preschool as very angry. She fell on the floor in a tantrum and slapped the face of the teacher who tried to pick her up. (She was only two years old.) Ashley was very independent, verbal, and got along with other children most of the time. It was when the teacher or mother wanted her to do something she didn't agree to that sparks flew. Not only is the Mars inconjunct willful Pluto, the endurance level is so high it can outlast the adult's patience and turn into an outright war. If given a time out, Ashley would continue to get up in spite of continued admonitions to sit down. Eventually she would remove her shoes and throw them. As a last resort, she would pee her pants and throw them, too! Wow! I remember one little boy who insisted in getting off his bed at naptime to go to the doorway to look for his mother. After putting him patiently on his bed 100 times, he peed all over the sheet and blanket so they had to be changed. Winning, to this persistent type of child, is more important than anything else.

If carried too far, this kind of persistence can develop into a full-blown oppositional disorder. This disorder can begin in a child as early as 3 years old and is manifested by disobedient, negativistic and provocative behavior. If the individual is thwarted, temper tantrums are likely. Even when the interests or state of well-being of the individual is involved, the child will still continue in her persistence. The behavior prevents the child from having pleasurable relationships.

An example of this scenario is found in Diamond's chart. She came to preschool at 4 years of age and adapted quickly. She had a tragic early childhood, losing her mother to violence, and was then placed with her grandmother. Soon it was apparent that Diamond had a problem following any directions. If there was a rule, she would break it. She was against any suggestion made to her; if asked do something she'd refuse; if asked to stop doing something, she insisted on continuing; she often threw chairs and cursed at the teacher. When she moved to kindergarten, the behavior continued until the teacher became desperate about what to do. A psychological evaluation was called for

Distractibility and Persistence   39

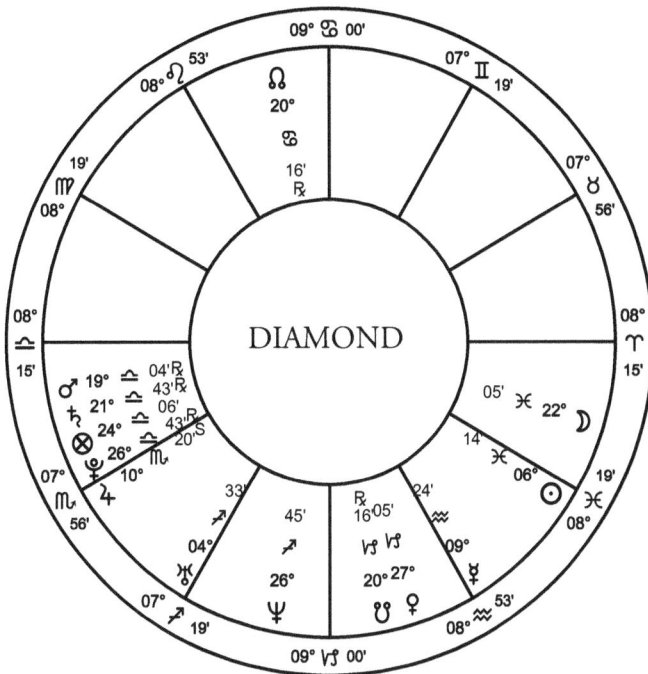

and eventually Diamond was given special placement in a setting that could help her. In her chart the Mars, Saturn, Pluto stellium in the 1st house is inconjunct the Moon. Her persistence level is high (70 points) while the distractibility falls in the normal range (45 points). The square between Venus and Pluto indicates the persistence problem was directed toward the area of social relationships.

A boy with the same stellium, Ronald, also had a tragic event early in life. In this case he lost his father who was sent to prison because of violent actions. He was raised by his mother. He was cautious on entering preschool but he adapted quickly. Different from the other little boys who wore jeans and sneakers, Ronald preferred trousers, shirts and shoes. He resembled a little man even at 3 years old. His high level of persistence (75 points) rapidly became obvious. His distractibility level was normal (40 points). He was very independent, highly intelligent and verbal but he liked to have his own way. He had complete control over his mother who always conceded to his wishes.

40 Kidwheels

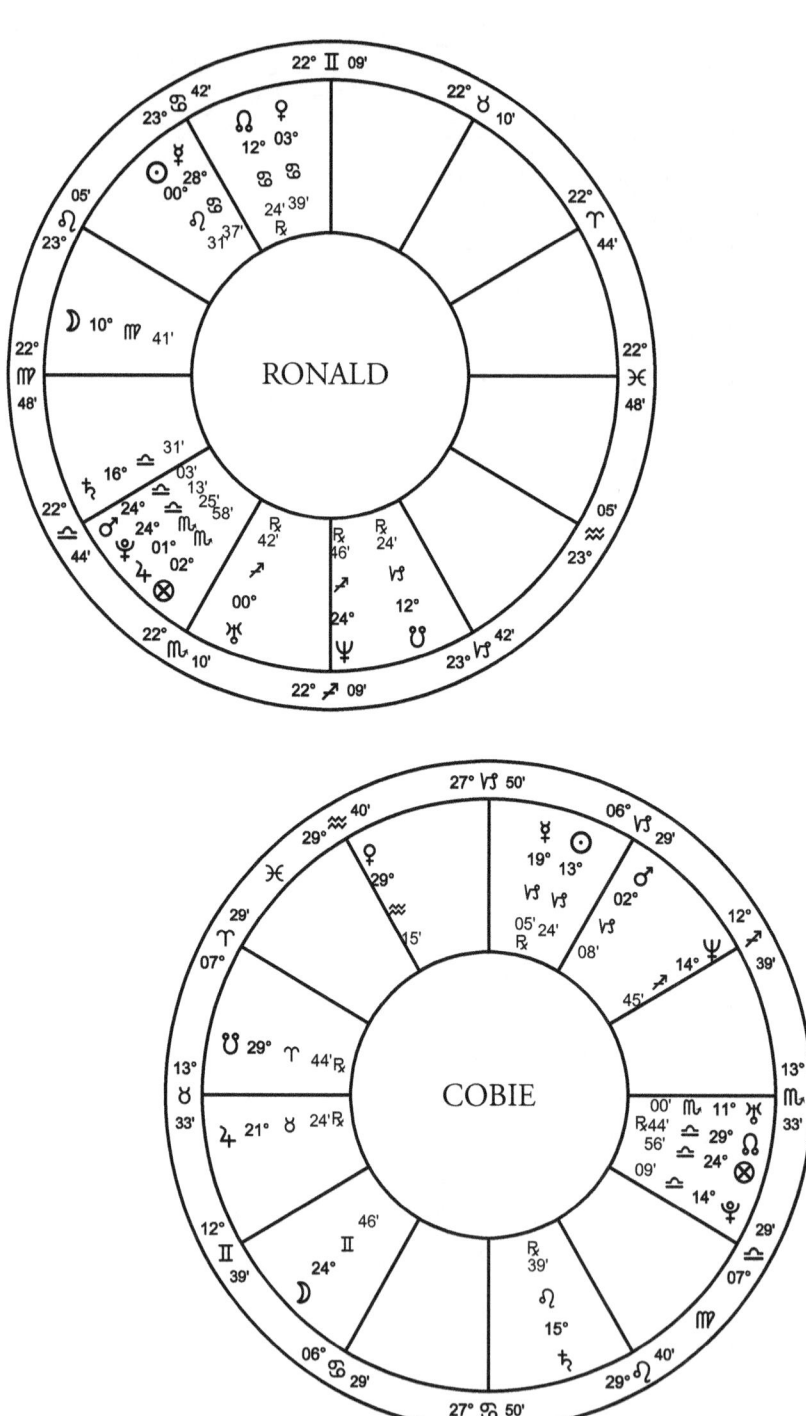

If pushed too far, he would have a tantrum, but as he grew older, he developed more control over his impulses. He liked dressing well and wearing expensive jewelry. His persistence and intelligence paid off for him. He obtained scholarships to Princeton and Columbia Universities and eventually obtained a law degree. He now works for a law firm back East and still wears expensive clothes and jewelry.

Cobie's chart also shows a high persistence level (85 points) with a normal range (40 points) in distractibility. She is well-balanced in three elements but lacks Water. She was not an emotional child and seldom responded in anger. Also, a highly intelligent girl, Cobie showed a lot of responsibility and was always helpful to the teacher and other children. She went on to get a college education and is now a social worker and a proud mother of four.

It is important to study persistence and distractibility as they relate to each other. Success in school and in life will be dependent on enough persistence to set goals and follow through to their completion. Sometimes a child will demonstrate both high distractibility along with high persistence. This child will be very sensitive to his environment and sense perceptions but when he becomes interested in a task, he will become so engrossed in it he can turn off his attention to the outside until the task is completed.

Chapter 5

Activity Level

"Can't you ever sit still?" the annoyed mother of a highly active child asks.

"Hurry up!" demands the father of a slow-moving child. "Must you always keep us waiting?"

These parents are reacting to the motor component of temperament. Activity level describes how much motion or energy the child shows during activities. Some children display lots of energy, needing space to run and climb. Other children seem calmer and have a lower energy output. They prefer quieter activities. The majority of children fall somewhere in between. They enjoy both active and quiet activities, moving easily from one to the other. By itself, activity level is not a problem; we expect children to be active. It is in the extremes of high or low activity that problems arise. Parental management becomes more difficult. If paired with other temperamental attributes, such as high persistence or high distractibility, the problem is magnified.

High Activity Level

Children with high activity level are always on the go. Even as babies, they wiggle, squirm and resist dressing. As toddlers, they are busy exploring and climbing; they prefer running to walking. Long trips are like keeping a young race horse boxed up too long: they soon bolt. Also, like a bull in a china shop, they dash about running into people and things, causing breakage and hurting themselves. No wonder parents get irritated. Such unrestrained exuberance may be misinterpreted as disobedience, the subject of continuous scolding and punishment. Self-esteem is eroded. A shortage of space and time to release this high energy exacerbates the problem. (Note: as with high distractibility, high activity can be mistaken for ADD by parents and teachers.)

The high activity level in a chart has the following signature (See Worksheet #6 in the Appendix):

Points Factors
30   Mars aspects to Ascendant
25   Mars in Aries, Gemini, Sagittarius
20   Mars aspects to Jupiter, Sun, Uranus
15   Sun in Aries, Sagittarius
10   Sun aspects to Jupiter
100

If the total number of points is below 50, the child falls in the normal or average level of activity. Higher than 50 points indicates a high to extremely high level of activity. There are other factors that should also be taken into account:

1. When Mars has good aspects to Mercury, coordination is good; hard aspects indicate coordination is off and accidents are more likely.

2. Mars exalted in Capricorn can indicate athletic ability.

3. Mars in the Gauquelin Sector of the Ascendant can also indicate athletic ability.

4. Mars in hard aspects to Saturn can indicate possibility of broken bones.

5. Mars in hard aspects to Uranus is impulsive and can lead to accidents.

Highly active children require more adult supervision than their less active peers. There is always a higher potential for accidents. High activity is also found more often in boys than girls (although this may be changing). Culturally speaking, high activity is more rewarded in

44   Kidwheels

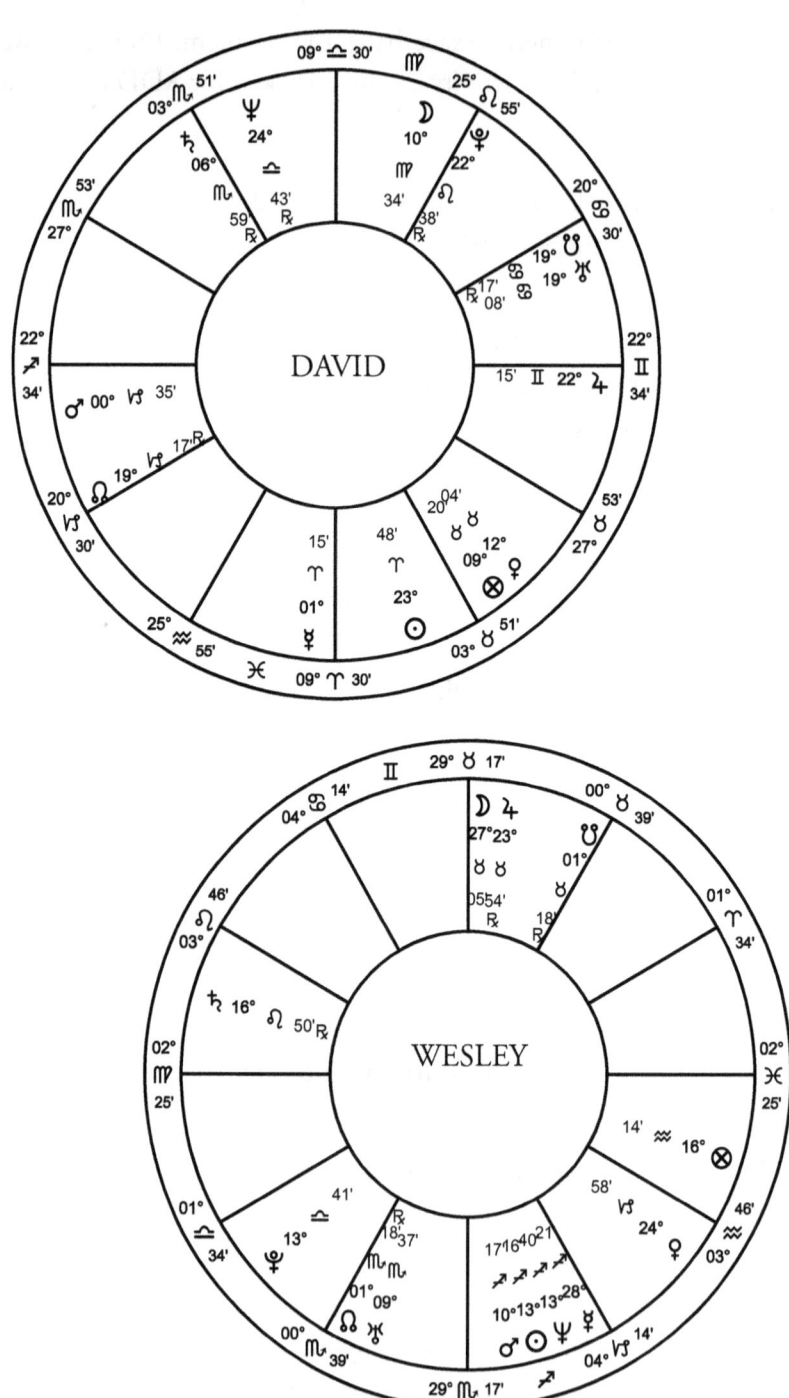

boys because of our society's emphasis on sports. However, having a high activity level does not necessarily equate to talent for sports.

Hayden's high activity level falls in the normal range at 30 points. Clara's level is also normal but a little higher at 40 points. They have both taken karate lessons and engaged in regular active games at school. There have been no problems in this area.

I've included the chart of my son, David, because he is a good example of how a high activity level (70 points) can translate into adult life. He is also a successful athlete. He was highly active from the beginning. He walked at nine months but he preferred running. He couldn't get through a doorway without bumping his head. He was heavily into sports as soon as he was old enough: bowling, baseball and handball. As an adult he skis cross-country, scuba dives, does back-packing hikes in the mountains, and has had a successful career as a handball player. (He was recently ushered into the US Handball Hall of Fame. Well, a mother is entitled to brag a little, isn't she?) Retired from IBM, he now is a coach of a university handball team. In addition to the high activity level, his Mars is exalted in Capricorn in the Gauquelin sector. Pluto in exact trine to his Ascendant gives him the endurance to outperform even younger players. The Mercury square Mars resulted in accidents involving his shoulder, one requiring surgery.

High activity level in a child can lead to accomplishment if it is channeled properly. These children need space to run off their energy. If they are cooped up in an apartment most of the day, for instance, a trip to the park is advisable. On a long trip, frequent stops are needed for a run around. Any form of sports should be introduced as early as possible. There are early gym and movement classes for preschoolers which can be beneficial.

To examine charts of other highly active children, we'll begin with Wesley. His activity level was high at 85 points. His mother described him as a highly active baby. He wriggled and squirmed when being dressed, and kicked off his blankets in bed. He walked at seven and a

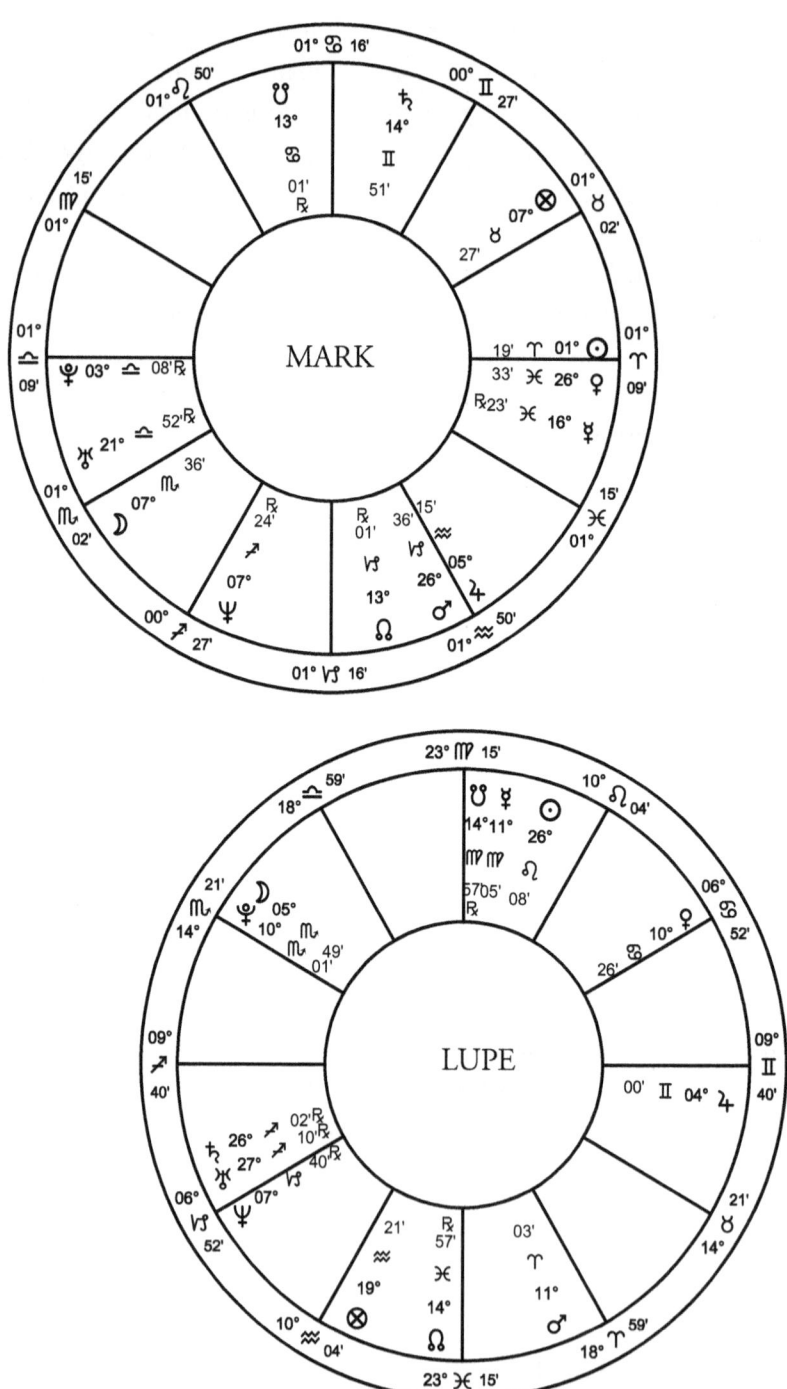

half months. Wesley enjoyed lots of physical activity at preschool and he developed excellent motor skills (Mars trine Saturn). Fortunately, his long attention span and persistence enabled him to complete tasks at less active levels. He didn't make severe management demands on the teachers because his responses were mild, he was good-natured, and was of positive mood.

Mark is an example of a highly active child (75 points) who had problems because his high activity was paired with a negative mood and high persistence. He walked at ten months and was described by his mother as a very active baby. He liked to explore and try new things. He was also a dare-devil. When he saw a man on TV hurtling his motorcycle over barrels, Mark decided to try something similar on his bike. This resulted in a concussion and a broken clavicle. All at four years of age! Athletics was a good outlet for all his energy but he was encouraged to enter individual competition rather than team sports. He was difficult to manage, not only because of his negative mood, but also by his tendency to angry and violent reactions when thwarted. Here is another case with Pluto involved. Not only is it conjunct his Ascendant but it also opposes the Sun/Venus conjunction and squares the MC. The Mars square Uranus aspect shows that he preferred to follow his own rules.

Lupe is an example of a highly active girl (80 points). She preferred active play with the boys to quieter play with the girls. She did not like to sit too long at group time either. Her high distractibility (80 points) interfered with her ability to focus for long. Her persistence level was in the normal range so she could complete tasks with many reminders by teachers. Fortunately, she had a very sunny nature being mostly Fire and Air.

Another example is Samuel who we met in Chapter 3. He has a level of 90 for high activity. The only thing that anchors him is having a Taurus Sun in the 1st house. As a baby he was very active, kicking the covers off, moving all over the crib. When he was in the crawling stage, he mostly got up on all fours and scampered like a puppy. At 18 months he was jumping in the pool, by three he'd taught himself to swim. Now in elementary school, he plays baseball, soccer, basketball and is an excellent bowler. He's highly distractible but persistence falls in the normal range. He can complete tasks, particularly if he is interested in them.

Low Activity

If the high activity child has problems with adults telling him to slow down, the low activity child faces the opposite problem—adults forever telling her to hurry up. While high activity children run into problems almost from birth, low activity children do not because they are easy to care for. The everyday tasks of dressing, feeding, bathing and changing are less demanding on their mother. The child moves at a slower speed and seems content to sit quietly in one place while mother goes about her business. What a blessing! As the child grows older, however, these assets turn into liabilities. The family grows impatient with the child's apparent inability to be ready for outings, dress for school, or complete a meal on time. Hurrying and scolding have just the opposite effect. In fact, a most common result is a sibling taking over for the child. Low activity leads to inertia as the child passively accepts others doing for her what she should be learning for herself. Unfortunately, the message to the child is "You are incompetent." She is deprived of the opportunity to develop independence and self-confidence. As she gets older the parents are amazed and annoyed at the child's apparent inability to function without a lot of prodding or assistance. Combinations with other traits such as slow adaptation, negative mood or high persistence leads to other problems such as dawdling, procrastination and oppositional behavior. Another problem for these children is that their slowness is often equated with dullness. The faster siblings and classmates tend to get the most attention while they are ignored. They require more attention and patience by adults for them to be able to shine in their own way. I measure low activity using the following steps (See Worksheet #6 in Appendix C):

Points Factors
30   Mars in Leo, Scorpio, Taurus, Cancer
25   Neptune aspects to Ascendant
20   Saturn aspects to Ascendant
15   Mars aspects to Saturn, Neptune
10   Bowl pattern
100

In this case, below 50 is normal or average while those with the higher numbers would indicate low activity (the higher the number, the lower the activity level). I found many low active children with the bowl pattern in their charts. This may be because the bowl pattern individual is so self-contained and fixed in style. Neptune aspects are frequent because they drain the energy when aspected to Mars or the Ascendant.

Hayden, while normal in high activity, has a low level of activity (65 points) and spends much of his time in quiet pursuits like reading, computer games and Lego projects.

Clara falls in the normal range for both high and low levels of activity which means she can move easily between high and low level activities.

Worksheet #6: Activity Levels

NAME: Hayden

High Activity Level

Examine the chart and assign points as follows:

Points Factors

Points	Factors	
30	Mars aspects to Ascendant	0
25	Mars in Aries, Gemini, Sagittarius	0
20	Mars aspects to Sun, Jupiter, Uranus	20
15	Sun in Aries or Sagittarius	0
10	Sun aspects to Jupiter	10
	Total	**30**

Notes: Score below 50 is normal activity level; above 50 is high activity level.

Hayden's score falls in the normal range for activity level. He did play some T-Ball and took karate lessons but is not very active. Given his choice, he prefers quiet activities.

Low Activity Level

Examine the chart and assign points as follows:

Points Factors

Points	Factors	
30	Mars in Leo, Scorpio, Taurus, Cancer, Pisces	30
25	Neptune aspects to the Ascendant	0
20	Saturn aspects to the Ascendant	20
15	Mars aspects to Neptune, Saturn	15
10	Bowl Pattern	0
	Total	**65**

Notes: Score below 50 falls in normal activity level; above 50 is low activity level.

Hayden spends much time with his Lego projects, computer games, and reading. With his low activity level, he prefers quieter activities.

Worksheet #6: Activity Levels

NAME: Clara

High Activity Level

Examine the chart and assign points as follows:

Points	Factors	
30	Mars aspects to Ascendant	30
25	Mars in Aries, Gemini, Sagittarius	0
20	Mars aspects to Sun, Jupiter, Uranus	0
15	Sun in Aries or Sagittarius	0
10	Sun aspects to Jupiter	10
	Total	**40**

Notes: Score below 50 is normal activity level; above 50 is high activity level.

Clara falls in the normal range for activity level. She has taken dancing lessons but prefers more sedentary activities.

Low Activity Level

Examine the chart and assign points as follows:

Points	Factors	
30	Mars in Leo, Scorpio, Taurus, Cancer, Pisces	30
25	Neptune aspects to the Ascendant	0
20	Saturn aspects to the Ascendant	0
15	Mars aspects to Neptune, Saturn	0
10	Bowl Pattern	0
	Total	**30**

Notes: Score below 50 falls in normal activity level; above 50 is low activity level.

Clara also falls in the normal range. She can move easily between low or high activities.

Kidwheels

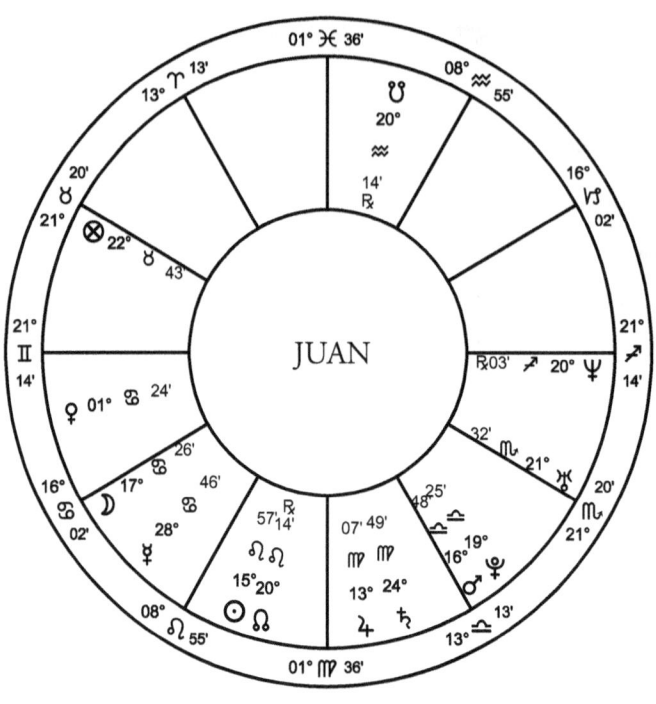

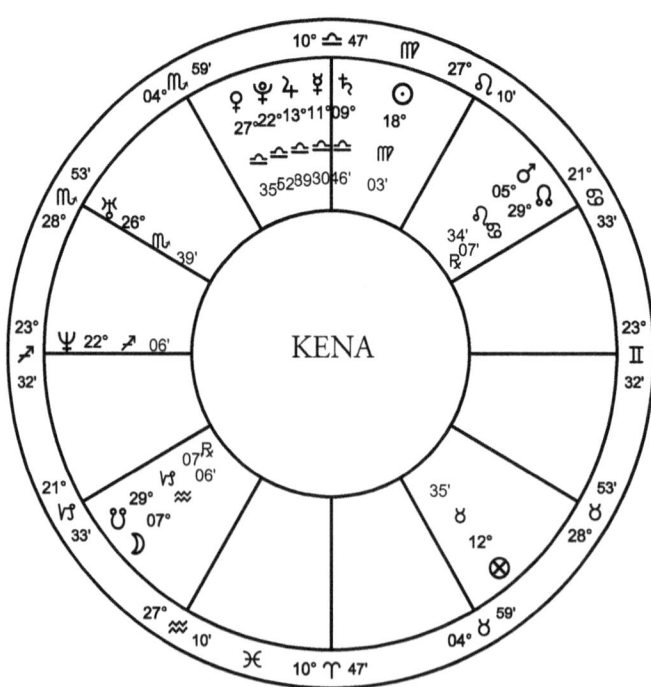

Juan's chart provides a good example of a boy with a low level of activity (70 points). His mother described him as a low active child who was easy to care for. She further said he was highly sensitive, adapted slowly to new things and had a negative mood. He entered preschool at two and by eight years he was still rather shy, preferring to spend his time in quiet activities with one or two friends. In elementary school, he was designated as mentally gifted. All the planets in his bowl pattern fill the Northern hemisphere making him a very private, self-contained boy.

Kena is another example of low activity level (80 points). In addition to her bowl pattern, her level of response is the Type 4. She was a deliberate, certain child who approached everything in a cautious way, especially with Mercury conjunct Saturn. With Neptune on the Ascendant she seemed to move in a fog. The high level of Earth/Air (83) contributed to a sense of detachment and a lack of emotionalism paired with her Aquarius Moon. Fortunately, her positive mood contributed to her being well-liked by other children. In fact, many of her friends became her "helpers" when it came to transitions and completing tasks. Children like this don't get the attention and rewards from teachers because they tend to get lost in the crowd.

April's low activity level was 75 points. Her mother described her as being easy to dress as an infant, quiet, staying where she was placed. At school she was the same way, being a cautious deliberate Type 4 child.

Adrienne is a good example of how inadequate a "Your Gemini Child" approach to interpretation would be in describing her. As a preschool child, she was difficult to manage because of her low activity level (75 points) combined with high distractibility. With the Sun/Moon conjunction trine to Pluto and inconjunct to Uranus, she could act out explosively when not given her way. Pluto also is square to her Venus which increased her difficulty in social relations with teachers and other children. She sucked her thumb continually. It was finally

54   Kidwheels

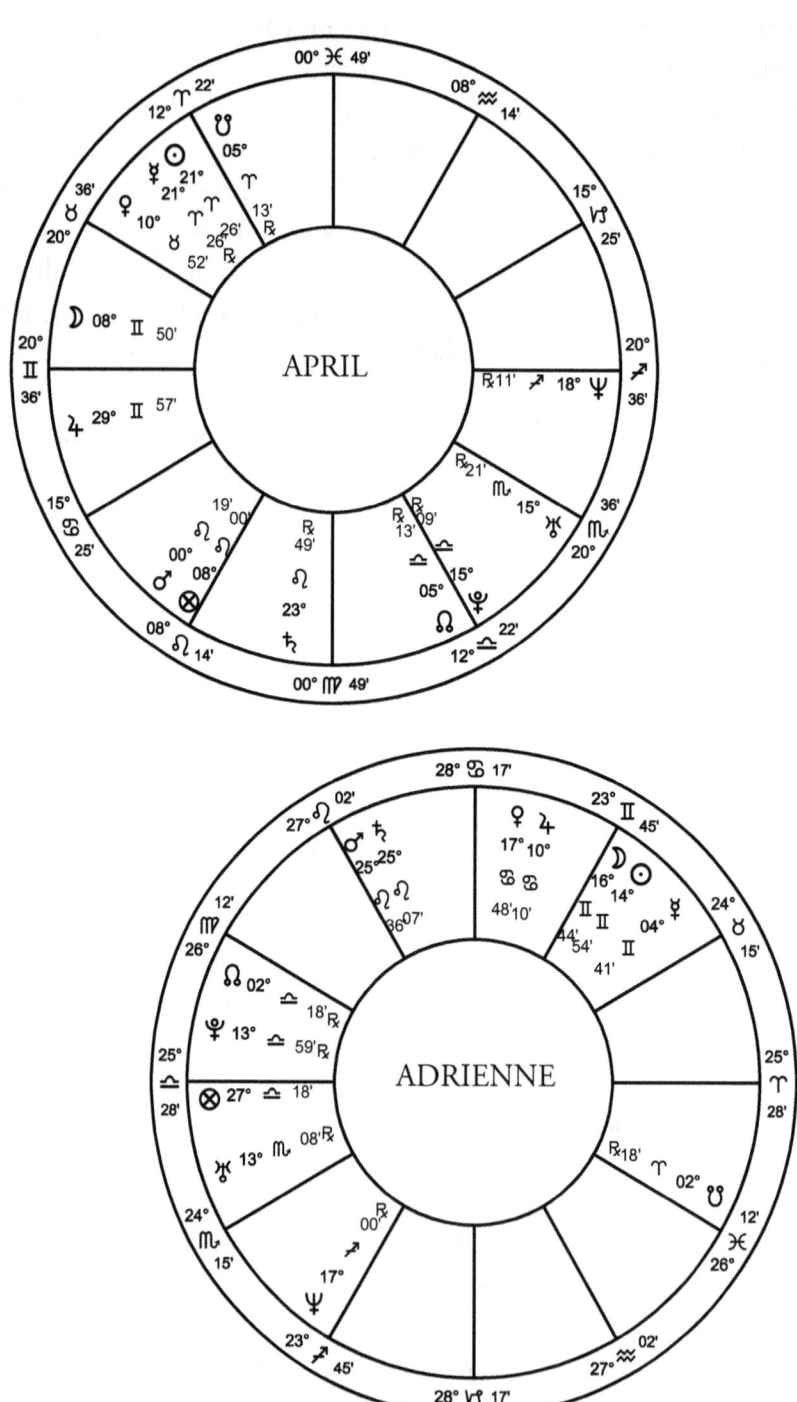

necessary to counsel the mother that her inconsistent handling of the child was adding to, if not creating the problem.

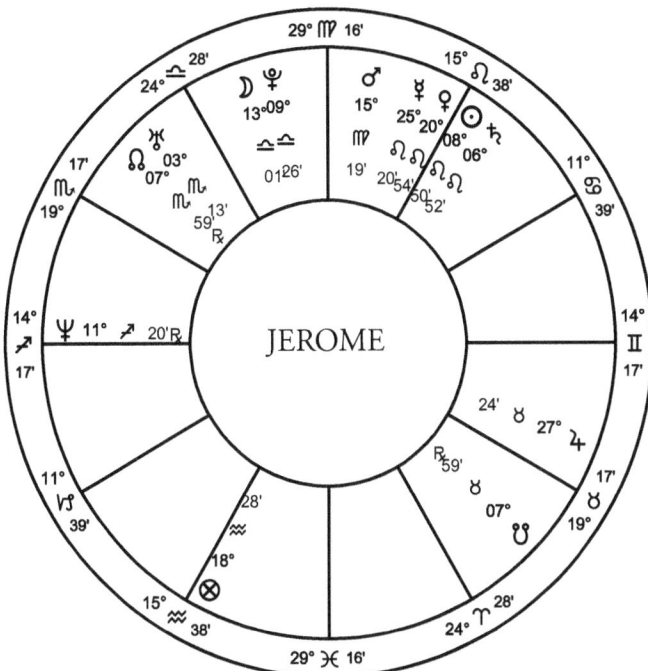

Jerome was a child with low activity (70 points) but normal in most of the other components. His mood was positive as he took his time to adapt to the school routine. While he participated in some of the more active activities, he was quite fixed on the quiet choices he made. With Neptune on the Ascendant, trine the Sun, sextile the Moon and square his Mars, he seemed to live in his own little world most of the time.

Activity is the last of the temperamental components. The next step is to bring all the elements of temperament together to determine the "Temperamental Type". Since these patterns of temperament persist over time, it is essential that caretakers be advised of helpful strategies that will promote the optimal development of those in their care.

Chapter 6

Temperamental Types

"Our brain is a sort of computer which has temperament for its hardware and character for its software."
                                                                David Keirsey

In their longitudinal study of temperament, Thomas, Chess and Birch defined three categories of behavioral types. These were called the easy child, the slow-to-warm-up child, and the difficult child. Each group demonstrates a unique pattern of traits as shown in the table below.

Temperament characteristic	Type of temperament		
	Easy	**Slow-to-warm-up**	**Difficult**
Activity level	Varies	Low to moderate	Varies
Rhythmicity	Very regular	Varies	Irregular
Distractibility	Varies	Varies	Varies
Approach/ withdrawal	Approaches readily	Withdraws at first	Withdraws
Adaptability	Very adaptable	Slowly adaptable	Slowly adaptable
Attention span/ persistence	High or low	High or low	High or low
Intensity of reaction	Low or mild	Mild	Intense
Sensitivity	High or low	High or low	High or low
Quality of mood	Positive	Slightly negative	Negative

Source: Thomas A, Chess S, Birch AG. 'The Origin of Personality', *Scientific American*.

Continuing research has accepted and expanded on these concepts. Forty percent of babies fall into the easy child category. Fifteen percent of babies are categorized as slow-to-warm-up. Ten percent are termed "difficult". The other thirty-five percent represent various combinations. For example, high distractibility can be paired with high or low activity, positive or negative mood, low or high intensity of reactions. The highly persistent child can also be paired with various combinations of traits. Putting all of these possible combinations into a convenient table is impossible. Knowing each component well will help in describing various pairings to parents. For instance, in studying Clara's chart we find that she could be described as an easy child. Most of her traits fall into the normal range; mood, adaptability, activity level, approach/withdrawal and so forth. Around the age of two, on her first Mars return, her high level of persistence became problematic. Not getting her way about choices she made produced tantrums and high, intense emotional outbursts. This required special handling by the parents. Because they were forewarned in the analysis of her chart, they were prepared with strategies to handle the situation.

Another example is the highly active child paired with positive mood and distractibility. He will be less of a problem to the parents than the highly active child paired with persistence and high intense reactions. High distractibility paired with low activity, as in the case of Adrienne, led to a low frustration tolerance when she couldn't complete something right away. This often brought on a tantrum. In Kena's case, her low activity level paired with her slow tempo of adjustment made her appear dull when she was, in fact, intelligent. Because she was slow to move, other children often took charge of her to get her moving.

All of these variations make each child unique. It should be the responsibility of the astrologer to understand this uniqueness when counseling parents. Parents need to understand that the child is born with a temperament which determines how they behave. Temperament is also relatively stable over time. Parental efforts to control or change it can have negative consequences for the child's development. What is needed is the parent's loving acceptance and support for the child's temperamental traits and individual needs. Parents and caregivers should understand the following:

Management strategies that worked with one child may not be effective with another.

- Parents need to pay attention and respect the individual child's needs.

- Parents should seek resources that will help them understand their child's temperament and strategies that can help to manage the individual child.

- Parents should be sensitive to the individual characteristics of their child.

- Parents should be flexible in responding to those characteristics.

- Parents should avoid applying any negative labels to the child.

- Parents should work together with their child to create harmony in the home.

- Parents should provide an environment where every child can be successful.

It would be beneficial if the astrologer had lists of resources such as books, magazines, and websites that parents could refer to for help in understanding temperament. In depth counseling with parents will follow in a later volume.

What follows in the next few pages are descriptions of temperamental types, their characteristics, and management strategies for each.

THE EASY CHILD

Characteristics
Regular in body functions
Positive mood
Low to mild reactions
Rapidly adaptable
Positive approach to anything new

Management

Handling of this child is easy for mother. Most of these children grow up to be well-adjusted adults. The only possible conflict arises if the standards of the school (or other environment) are in sharp contrast to those of the parents. In this case, the child may become defensive, withdraw, or become aggressive. Usually the child can be flexible and adopt behaviors appropriate to each situation. It is important to understand the values and child-rearing practices of the parents. Most helpful is advising parents to encourage independence because this child will easily follow others and pick up habits of stronger children.

- Easy children are easy to neglect. Parents need to pay attention to them.
- The easy child gets lost in the crowd; make sure they are heard as much as their more active, attention-getting siblings.
- Don't let them spend too much time in front of the television because it's easier and less demanding. They need enough time with parents just like the ones who demand it.
- Don't let the easy child become the neglected child.

THE SLOW-TO-WARM-UP CHILD

Characteristics
Low to moderate activity level
Initial withdrawal responses to anything new
Slow adaptability
Negative mood
Mild reactions
May or may not be distractible or persistent

Management

These children move into new activities slowly, gradually and steadily unless they are rushed. If pushed or coaxed, they will retreat, withdraw and begin avoidance maneuvers. They prefer to stand and watch others for a period of time before joining in. This period can vary from a few weeks to months. They're not withdrawn but are observant and are slowly assimilating the environment. Parents need to be patient and willing to wait. They should give many opportunities to re-experience any new food, activity or situation without pressuring the child to act or join in. If pushed or treated impatiently, she may resort to negativism, avoidance, even tantrums. The parents should not give up offering the food or activity because this prevents her from developing the opportunity to adapt. Once the child feels comfortable with the new experience; she will gradually behave like the rest of the children. However, changes in routine or environment bring the child back to square one where she has to begin the process all over again. As she grows older, the parents can help her to recognize the pattern and thus adjust more quickly.

- Prepare child in steps for new experiences.
- Give child time to respond to adults (don't jump in to answer for them).
- Translate your child's behavior to new people.

- Prepare child for changes or new experiences.
- Don't try to change the child, accept them for who they are.
- Be patient.
- Use positive discipline—use guidance and coaching.

THE DIFFICULT CHILD

Characteristics
Irregular in bodily functions
Negative responses to anything new
Slow to adapt to anything new
Negative mood
Intense reactions
Can be high or low in persistence

Management

Expect this child to withdraw from anything new such as new foods, new people, new situations. He will eventually adapt if not pushed; he has to have repeated exposures before he can adapt positively. He hesitates to engage in organized activities and has difficulty each time a new demand is made. Mothers often have feelings of self-doubt, guilt, anxiety and helplessness. Parents often express anger, frustration, and exhaustion from power struggles with this child. They need to understand that he requires extra patience, guidance and time. However, parents can become effective by developing strategies and communication skills that will help the child learn to be more self-controlled and cooperative. This temperamental type was found to be most likely to develop behavior problems if not properly handled. Strong insistence on compliance with demands increases negative responses and leads to increasing defiance and power struggles. Appeasement of the child leads to a child tyrant. Consistent approaches that are calm but firm are required.

- Avoid name-calling and labeling.
- Focus on strengths and voice praise for cooperation.
- Give the child options so he is part of the decision-making process.
- Be patient and empathize while interpreting temperamental traits to the child.
- Keep to a predictable schedule, warn ahead of any changes in routine.
- Warn the child well ahead of transitions that are coming.
- Help the child learn self-control when he tantrums. Give him time and space to cool down before talking to him.
- Avoid power struggles. Make sure he knows what the rules are and the consequences for infractions. Carry out the consequences calmly and matter-of-factly while making the child responsible for his behavior. This way you don't appear to be the arbitrary dictator. He can't argue when it was HIS CHOICE to break the rules.
- Give him hope. You know he can make good choices. Next time will be better.

THE HIGHLY DISTRACTIBLE CHILD

Characteristics

Attention is easily drawn away by external events

Moves quickly from one activity to another

Short attention span

Loses things, forgets, doesn't put things away

Usually talkative

Persistence may be present or absent

Management

Use a patient, positive approach. The child can't really help himself and may be struggling with feelings of inadequacy. Use friendly reminders to encourage the child to return to a task. Since the attention span is short, frequent breathers are necessary. If the task is long, break it into smaller segments with short rests in between so he can be more motivated by small successes. Children can develop useful techniques to help themselves. For example, get into the habit of making check lists or use a timer. As the child gets older, he will need a quiet area with few distractions in order to do homework. Some children prefer quiet music in the background. At school, it's best if he's placed between quiet children. You can help by explaining to the teacher and to the child himself about his focus issues.

- Use a friendly, positive approach.
- Get the child on a consistent schedule. Let him participate in creating it.
- Create check lists. For example, a list on the bedroom door of things he needs to take with him. Use charts of routines to keep him on track.
- Be on the child's level to make eye contact when you need his full attention.

- Don't take over tasks your child needs to finish himself. This creates a dependency that deprives him of a sense of mastery which improves his self-esteem.
- Give the child praise on things completed.
- Your loving support will help him to see himself in a positive way.

PERSISTENT CHILD

Characteristics
Gets engrossed in any activity
Difficulty making transitions
Does not like to be interrupted or hurried
Often has tantrums or acts "stubborn"
Can be mild or intense in reactions
Can be high or low in activity level
May be selective in what she is persistent in
Can "nag" until she gets what she wants

Management

Don't reinforce the negative behavior by getting irritated or angry. Remain calm. Give the child options so she can be part of the decision-making process and give her a warning before transitions are made. Don't let the child become engaged in an activity if it is close to transition time. Do not engage in power struggles, react to tantrums, or show anger. If necessary, remove the child from the situation, give them time to cool down, and then talk to them. Make sure your expectations of the child's behavior are very clear. Be firm and consistent in your expectations and the consequences for the infractions. Follow-through is important. Be more persistent than the child. These children can exhaust you, so you need cooperation with the spouse who can take over. Being angry and impatient, or engaging in power struggles can result in the child developing an oppositional disorder. Remember that persistence is the hallmark of people who are successful. Breaking a child's will may make her obedient out of fear but it breaks that precious trust in your relationship to the child and creates resentment in its place. You don't have to always prove you're right. Teach the child ways to calm themselves.

- Reward persistence when it is appropriate.
- Find win/win solutions. Learn and teach the art of communication, negotiation and compromise with your child. This is a valuable life skill.
- Help the child with transitions and routines. By knowing what to expect, the child is less likely to resist.
- Set firm limits but also be willing to empathize with the child's feelings when she doesn't always get what she wants. She'll learn the resilience to survive disappointment.
- Develop a code word with the child you can use to remind her it's time to stop nagging.

THE CHILD WITH INTENSE REACTIONS

Characteristics
Explosive and loud emotional expression
Overreacts to frustration
Screams with excitement when happy
May include physical expression like jumping up and down, clapping hands
Has frequent "meltdowns"

Management

Children who have intense reactions can't help themselves. It doesn't do any good for parents to tell these children to stop feeling what they're feeling or to "calm down". Trying to talk them out of what they are feeling only makes it worse. Parents need to accept and empathise with the child's feelings and instead of telling them they are being melodramatic help them learn how to calm down. Parents can explore what the triggers are, and develop a "feeling" vocabulary so the child can express themselves better. They can help the child become more aware of their physical reactions, so they sense when the emotion is building up and learn how to cope with it. If the child is having a meltdown in a public place, it's best to remove her from the situation, not as punishment, but as an opportunity for space and time to cool down. With parents' help, the child will eventually learn more self-control by use of techniques that help them calm themselves.

- Teach the child words to use to express their feelings.
- Help them find ways to channel their emotional energy in productive ways such as exercise, deep-breathing, pounding a punching bag.
- Accept and empathize with their feelings. This lets them know you are listening and that you care.

- Avoid stressful situations that can act as triggers, such as becoming over-scheduled or over-tired.
- Help them be more aware of how their intense emotions can have an adverse effect on others.
- Help them to recognize when they need to take a break.

HIGHLY ACTIVE CHILD

Characteristics
Moves quickly and frequently
More apt to break things
More likely to have injuries
More likely to collide with other children
May have mild or intense reactions
May be distractible or persistent

Management

The highly active child requires vigilant supervision to prevent him from getting into dangerous situations. He needs plenty of opportunity for motor activity and frequent breaks from situations that require him to sit for long periods of time. High activity can become irritating to adults so it is important for parents to maintain a cheerful attitude towards the noise, turmoil and breakage being created. Eventually all that energy can be channeled into sports.

- Incorporate exercise in every day routines.
- Give him age-appropriate tasks so he can be a "helper".
- Limit television.
- Get him outdoors to burn up energy.
- Give him choices.

- Develop "stop" signals to indicate when it's time to slow down.
- Use consistent discipline.
- Develop a quiet bed routine to help him settle down.
- Use nutritional snacks rather than sugary ones.

THE CHILD WITH LOW ACTIVITY

Characteristics
Slow moving
Content to stay in place for long periods
Slow to respond, make transitions, complete tasks
Chooses activities that don't require physical effort
May be slow-to-warm-up or persistent

Management

The child with low activity level needs plenty of warning in order to complete tasks before transitions. The child is easily overshadowed by faster-moving, more verbally responsive children. Make a point not to overlook her. Patience is required because pushing them only makes them dawdle more. Often these children are assumed to be slow intellectually as well. Don't make that judgment or it can shape your approach to the child and become a self-fulfilling prophecy. Another problem appears if others rush in to complete the task for the child, preventing her from developing self-help skills. Low activity level children need to be encouraged to engage in physical activities.

- Avoid labeling your child with negative terms like "slowpoke".
- Allow the child to complete a task without pushing or taking over.

- Incorporate some physical activity in daily routine, such as walking or riding a bike.
- Praise the child when tasks are completed.
- Being active with your child strengthens the relationship. Take a walk together.
- Explain to your child that activity reduces the risk of future health issues. Physical activity doesn't mean they have to be engaged in sports or be on a team. Slow children often feel inadequate in this area which can lower their self-esteem. Don't nag the child. Find useful ways to act as reminders, such as using a timer.

Chapter 7

Goodness of Fit and the Parental Axis

"Any temperamental attribute may become either an asset or a liability to a child's development, depending on whether the caregivers recognize what type of approach is best suited for that child."

Stella Chess, MD

"You cut the jacket to fit the person, you do not cut the person to fit the jacket."

Med Jones, President of International Institute of Management

Goodness of Fit

The "goodness of fit" model was first proposed by Thomas, Chess and Birch (1968) and later elaborated on by Thomas and Chess (1999). According to this model, when a child's temperamental type is compatible with the environment, a goodness of fit occurs and development proceeds in a positive manner. If the child's temperament clashes with the environment, there is a "poorness of fit" in which development proceeds in a negative manner leading to maladaptive functioning. The authors also gave importance to the beliefs and demands of the child's culture and socioeconomic group. Their new approach differed greatly from the psychoanalytical and behavioristic theories in wide use at the time. For Thomas, Chess and Birch, bi-directional interactions between children and their parents influenced their behaviors. A poorness of fit could lead to pathological functioning but this is not due to some unconscious pathological pattern. Rather, a child is born with a "vulnerability", such as high distractibility, which meets with negative, harsh judgment and punitive behavior by a caregiver. The expectations and demands to "pay attention" and complete a given task are beyond the capabilities of the child, creating stress and maladaptive behavior.

Astrologically, discovering whether there is a "good fit" or a "bad fit" between child and environment requires a thorough analysis of the parental axis, the 4th and 10th houses.

Parental Axis

> *"My mother protected me from the world and my father threatened me with it."*
>
> Quentin Crisp, *The Naked Civil Servant* (1968).

The parental axis represents the child's experience of being parented which includes both nurturing and discipline. This axis reminds us that both parents provide love, nurturing, tenderness, affection and closeness. At the same time, they set boundaries and limitations with some form of discipline. A structure is built based on the beliefs, morals and values that are filtered through the parents' culture. Various cultures have their own versions of what they consider proper child-rearing practices which are passed onto the parents. For example, some cultures encourage independence while others favor cooperation. These values are represented by the 10th house. The child's experience of authority here will color future interactions with authority figures. The 10th house also represents the goals and expectations the parents set for the child's later achievement.

The child is born at the Ascendant, the first contact with the outer world. The 4th house represents the environment the child will experience from birth to around two years when the first Mars return will push the child from the symbiotic relationship with mother into the first step on the path to individuation. Much of what happens in this Lunar Period has a profound effect on the stages of development that follow. The 4th house is the foundation of the course of development which follows, and therefore demands the greatest scrutiny and analysis. Such analysis requires a good understanding of the various processes that are taking place in the first two years of a child's life.

Analyzing the Fourth House

Consider first the basic elemental interaction taking place between the child and the 4th house. To quote Arroyo (1975), "On the level of normal experience, any relationship may be viewed as an interaction of two energy fields." (p.145) If the elements are in harmony, the two people feed each other's energy field. Another possibility is one person blocking the flow of energy of the other, creating frustration. With a compatible combination, there is a feeling of satisfaction and wholeness. An incompatible combination leads to a feeling of depletion and fragmentation. He goes on to say, "A child will automatically gravitate to the parent who feeds his magnetic field." This explains why children in the same family often have a better relationship with one parent over the other.

In Hayden's case we have a Cardinal/Water, slow-to-warm-up child with Libra on the 4th house cusp and Scorpio intercepted. Airy Venus in Gemini in the 10th house indicates his stay-at-home father was the parent he interacted with the most. Both parents are Scorpios with their Suns supporting Hayden's Cancer Sun and Moon from the 4th house. Importantly, Hayden's Venus in Gemini is supported by Dad's Gemini Ascendant and Mom's Gemini Moon. Both parents also have Venus in Libra supporting Hayden's 4th house.

This is not an emotional family. The parents may not always understand Hayden's shyness but they are there to support and encourage him. They may not express emotions freely but they communicate them through words, through quiet conversations with Hayden. He, in turn, is able to express his feelings openly, knowing they will be accepted by his parents. I consider this to be a pretty good "fit".

In Clara's case, we find a Cardinal/Air, persistent child with Aquarius on the 4th house cusp. The ruler, Saturn, is at 24 Virgo which conjuncts both parents' Uranus. This creates some tension which will probably manifest in Clara's choices of friends. The Air element is well supported by Mom's Gemini Moon and Dad's Gemini Ascendant, so again, there is a good fit between child and parent emphasized by verbal communication and nurturing interactions.

Attachment

A second consideration when analyzing the 4th house is the attachment process. During the first nine months of infancy, the child develops a specific preference for the primary caretaker, usually the mother. The baby looks to this person for security, protection and comfort and shows anxiety and unhappiness when separated from this figure. The seminal work of John Bowlby (1969), later expanded upon by Mary Ainsworth (1978), demonstrated that these early emotional bonds have a huge impact on future relationships that continue throughout life. Attachment, as an evolutionary factor, increases the child's chance of survival by keeping mother and child close together. Bowlby stated that the primary bond is formed between mother and child during the first 18 months of development. This pattern of interaction remains relatively stable over time until one or the other makes a concerted effort to change it. The baby begins to form attachments with other significant figures around nine months such as fathers, siblings and grandparents. The more figures available to the child for bonding, the less stress is felt if tragedy strikes. This was the value of the extended family. The primary attachment is most significant because, while it remains virtually unconscious, it is how we learned to form bonds in the most emotionally intimate way. When we become involved as adults in an emotional relationship, many of the security, dependency needs are triggered from the unconscious patterns of this period without our understanding the connection.

There are many factors that influence these attachments. The mother's consistent, rapid responses to the baby's needs aids in the growth of a sense of dependability and trust. Ainsworth labelled this as a "secure attachment" which occurs in the majority of cases. When the infant cannot depend on the mother to fulfill its needs, an insecure attachment called ambivalent or resistant occurs. In this situation, the child is anxious, insecure and angry. When the caregiver is abusive or neglectful, an avoidant attachment occurs in which the child is emotionally distant and does not explore much. A later attachment style was added by Main and Solomon (1986) called "disorganized attachment" in which the mother is very inconsistent and confused about her parenting practices. The child is depressed, angry, passive and unresponsive. His or her behavior may seem dazed and confused. Forms of attachment other than secure have a negative impact on the child's development and later behaviors.

As Bruce Scofield presents in his developmental model in *The Circuitry of the Self* (2001), the mother/child bond is critical. It is symbolized by the Moon and its configurations with the planets. He stresses the vulnerability of the infant to imprints during the Lunar Period which covers the first two years of life and includes the first Mars Return; this period lasts from birth to around 18 months to 2 years when the child is pushed out of its symbiotic relationship with the mother in order to establish a separate sense of self. Aspects to the Moon by inner planets are not as traumatic, he states (p.113). Those of the outer planets, including Saturn, particularly the hard aspects, can indicate disturbances formed in the early years. My work with both children and adult charts substantially agrees with the delineations and examples he gives in his book.

To enlarge on Scofield's model, I want to introduce an additional result of the mother/child bond: the child's ability to perform in preschool. The following is based on a study by the University of Harvard's School of Education called the Preschool Project. I covered this topic in my article 'Child and Parent' in the book *Web of Relationships* edited by Joan McEvers (1992) which includes charts from my files to illustrate how the early attachment to the mother influences later adult relationships. "Why Some 3-Year Olds Get As- and Some Get Cs" by Maya Pines (covering this project) can be found in the book *As the Tree is Bent*, edited by Robert H. Anderson and Harold G. Shane (1971). The purpose of the project, directed by Prof. Burton L. White, was to determine what constitutes competence in 3-year-olds in preschool and what maternal interactions contributed to the child's excellence. These were called "A" children. A parallel group, called "C" children, were found to be inept in their performance. The average, the "B" children, were not included in the study. By studying the child's performance in school along measurable lines in conjunction with observations of the mother/child interactions at home, the researchers came up with five prototypes of mothers and their children.

I have adapted their labels in order to describe the mother/child bond based on planetary aspects to the Moon. In this manner I am describing the form of attachment as well as the influence of this attachment on the child's competence in acquiring skills in preschool and their relationships in adult life.

Moon/Jupiter Relationship

Jupiter aspecting the Moon in the child's chart describes the "Supermom". She spends time with her child carrying on a running dialogue labelling things. She not only buys him educational toys, she interacts by playing with him rather than leaving him alone. She encourages his thinking by talking and asking questions. Nurturing in this Jupiterian sense provides encouragement to grow and expand, to assimilate experience with a sense of mastery and achievement. Less concerned with details, she helps by building whole patterns of information, seeing the connections between things. The energy of Jupiter can provide the foundation of trust and optimism that encourages growth and expansion. The Supermom produces the all-around "A" child with a secure attachment and positive self-esteem who is ready to tackle challenges in the belief that he will succeed.

Negatively, Mom can carry her teaching roles to extremes. She can be so eager to help that she doesn't allow room for the child to initiate things himself. A strong pattern of dependency is created (found with hard aspects of Moon/Jupiter). Too much success can be as deleterious as too little. There may be an arrest at the emotional level and little impetus to move on to face new uncertainty and tasks to master. Mom's insistence that he is already the best at everything is far from realistic. He has built an internal model of the world with himself as

King, leaving him ill-equipped to handle competition and rejection in the real world. There may be a spoiled, self-centered arrogance that is difficult for others to accept. Without some form of limitations, the child may remain fixated at the narcissistic, egocentric stage of development. He may be an "A" child in performance but a "C" in social/emotional development. The charts of Hayden and Clara illustrate the Supermom.

Moon/Saturn Relationship

The "Zoo-Keeper" Mother, as defined by the Harvard study, manifests as abundance of Saturnine energy. She is highly organized and disciplined. While the child's basic needs may be met, emotionally he is pretty much on his own. He may have educational toys but he plays by himself. There is little interaction between mother and child so the child has a highly stereotyped way of behaving. There is not much in the way of spontaneity or freedom of action. Fear of intimacy is suggested which creates an insecure attachment particularly with the hard aspects. Even the softer aspects manifest as an aloofness, an emotional reserve which requires some time to overcome before trust can be established. Too much Saturn energy affecting the Lunar Period damages the self-esteem and creates a sense of alienation, separation and fear of abandonment. This is similar to the Insecure, avoidant attachment in which the mother is distant and disengaged. The child believes that her needs will not be met. As an adult there's a deep longing for close emotional contact that was missed in childhood, but the fear of rejection and abandonment stifles the ability to get those needs met. Sometimes the child will be an "underachiever", depending on others for approval and not reaching his full potential. Some may overcompensate by working harder to achieve success to fill the emotional vacuum.

Tom's chart shows that he is basically a Fire/Air temperament which fits well in the 4th house with Leo on the cusp and the ruler in Aries. The Jupiter trining the Moon shows his beginning with a strong

Goodness of Fit and the Parental Axis

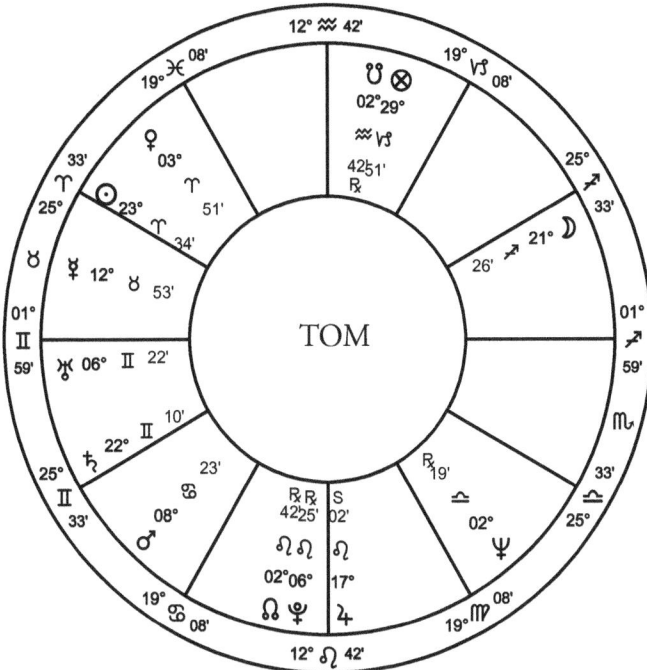

attachment to mother who acted as a Supermom. However, his parents divorced early on, and his mother was forced to place him and his brother in a foster home for a period of time. The Moon opposition to Saturn was traumatic for Tom as he experienced the separation as abandonment and felt isolated, alone and depressed. Even when he returned home, he was sent to a boarding school where he again felt isolated and abandoned. As an adult he is a very successful business man but maintains a close tie with his mother whom he idolizes. The Moon is in the 7th house ruled by Jupiter in the 4th house. His Venus opposite Neptune adds to the picture of idealization of women, and all of this manifests in his relationships with them. He married early, mostly for security reasons. Married three times in all, he longs for that close, warm, secure relationship to the mother he lost at an early age. Saturn manifests in his chart as a fear of intimacy and eventual abandonment. He is very generous financially to his partners but not emotionally. As soon as he begins to feel close to a woman, the tension becomes so overwhelming that he withdraws and begins to sabotage the relationship, eventually ending it.

Moon/Uranus Relationship

The "Overwhelmed Mother" is represented by Moon/Uranus aspects. She has so much going on in her life she doesn't have much time for her child. She may be working or just very involved in her activities and social life. Whatever the reason for her unavailability, the result is a child who is forced into early independence. What she learns is that others are unreliable and inconsistent. Sometimes her needs will be filled and other times they won't so she is left with uncertainty and unable to make safe predictions. With Uranus, the attachment is hit and miss so that the qualities of non-attachment grow out of the process. This is seen quite often in the children of military personnel where the family is frequently uprooted. The child learns that if she gets close to someone, the chances are she'll have to move. She learns to attach in a shallow way so the disruption in the bonding process will not be so painful. The same thing is happening in the bonding process with the mother, where one moment she may be hugging her and in the next moment, it's "don't bother me". In the softer aspects of Moon and Uranus, there's an emotional independence that requires freedom in close adult relationships. With the harder aspects there is an element of tension and unpredictability which is hard on the nerves. With Saturn there is a longing to attach but a fear of it. With Uranus you fear attachment itself because of the belief that others are unpredictable and unreliable. This mother usually produces a "C" child.

In Bill's chart we have the Overwhelmed Mother shown by the Moon conjunct Uranus and opposite the Sun. He is a Cardinal/Fire type and fits well in the Cardinal parent axis with the ruler Venus also in Aries.

Uranus in the 4th house shows the disruption in the home as the parents separated when he was quite young. Mother worked in the computer business and Dad was a successful comedy writer. Mother was quite busy with her career and had little time for her son. Dad remained in close contact with Bill and provided more of the

Goodness of Fit and the Parental Axis   79

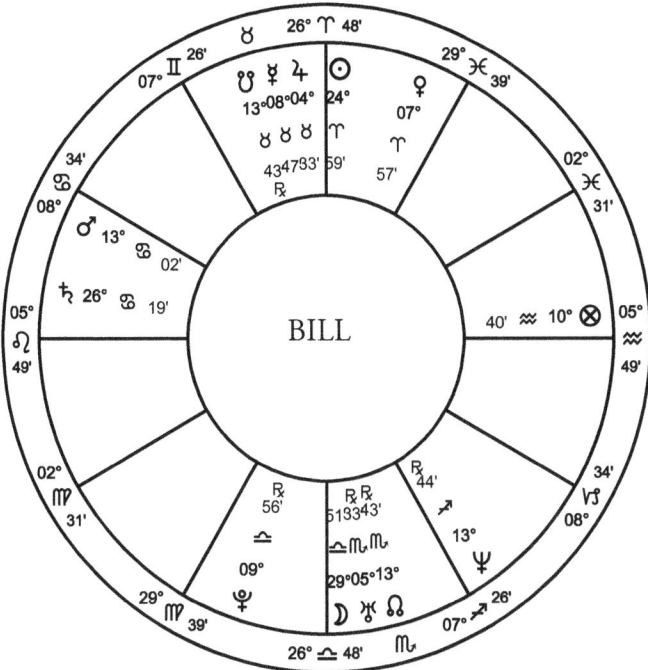

warmth and nurturing he needed. However, the T-square of Saturn with the Sun/Moon opposition shows that Bill still felt abandoned and isolated, particularly when his father remarried with a woman with a daughter close to his age. The ruler of the 4th house, Venus, is opposite Pluto which shows the tendency of the mother to be controlling which she defined as "being helpful". This opposition is square to Mars in another T-square which manifested in outbursts of violent temper by Bill towards his mother when she became too intrusive. Bill also had a high IQ but was an underachiever to the dismay of both parents. Though he admired his father, his feelings of inadequacy acted as a restraint on his own ability to succeed. On the surface, he could appear charming, outgoing, witty and articulate but he expressed little feeling and seemed emotionally distant from his family and friends.

Moon/Neptune Relationships

The "Almost Mother" involves Neptune. She may enjoy and accept the child but she's confused and frequently unable to understand his signals or respond to his needs. Quite often this mother is self-involved either because of illness, mental problems, alcohol or drugs abuse. She may be incapacitated by depression. At a very early age, the child begins to feel that mother needs him more than he needs her and he tries to help, taking on the parental role. Another possibility is the very permissive mother who doesn't know how to say "No", doesn't set boundaries, and the child has difficulty separating himself from her. There is a symbiotic immersion where the child has a problem in discerning the difference between his needs and hers. Eventually he creates an ideal picture of this relationship and goes through life looking for the "ideal woman" who will satisfy those unmet needs. He projects this illusion onto anyone who seems to fit the bill. After a time, reality shatters the illusion and he's left with disappointment, frustration and anger. In some cases, the child grows into a rescuer, searching for someone who needs to be rescued, or an alcoholic or drug abuser. Then he becomes the victim. The problem with Neptune is that it clouds the boundaries. He becomes convinced that if he tries hard enough and sacrifices enough, eventually he'll get what he needs. He may even try to find full immersion in a cause or a religion. The Almost Mother does okay at the beginning, but as the child grows she begins to fail. Eventually, he reaches a plateau and turns into a "B" child.

Jack's chart is difficult with all the planets packed into a tight wedge pattern, with no oppositions and both Sun and Moon squared by Neptune. In addition, the Moon is the final dispositor of the chart which increases its importance. With no oppositions, he is very subjective with little understanding or awareness of the "other". While Jack requires a partner to feel complete, he has no inner model for relating. He is a Cardinal/Water type which fits well with the Pisces 4th house. However, the rulers of both the 4th and 10th

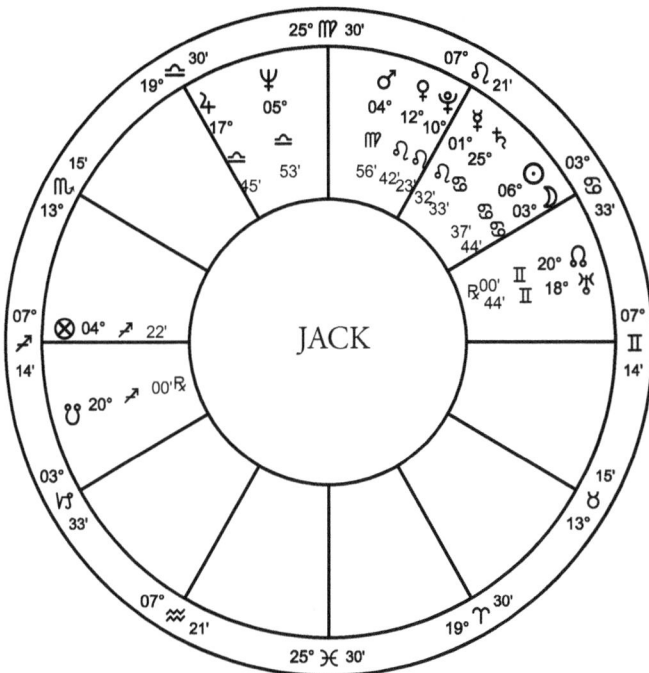

houses are unrelated as well as the 1st and 7th houses, ruled by the same planets. The attachment process was insecure and clouded by Neptune. Mother played a strong but unhealthy role in Jack's life. His father was critical and physically abusive. He was killed in a car crash when Jack was eight. Until the very critical age of twelve, he had his mother to himself and when she remarried, he bitterly resented it. His relationship with his wife has been abusive, possessive and intensely sexual. When his wife threatened to leave him, he tried to commit suicide. He became an alcoholic and eventually was arrested for dealing drugs.

Moon/Pluto Relationships

In the case of the "Smothering Mother", we see the force of Pluto's need to possess and dominate. This mother raises a child who is an "A" in learning ability but emotionally fearful and infantile. She is discontented with where the child is at any moment and is constantly

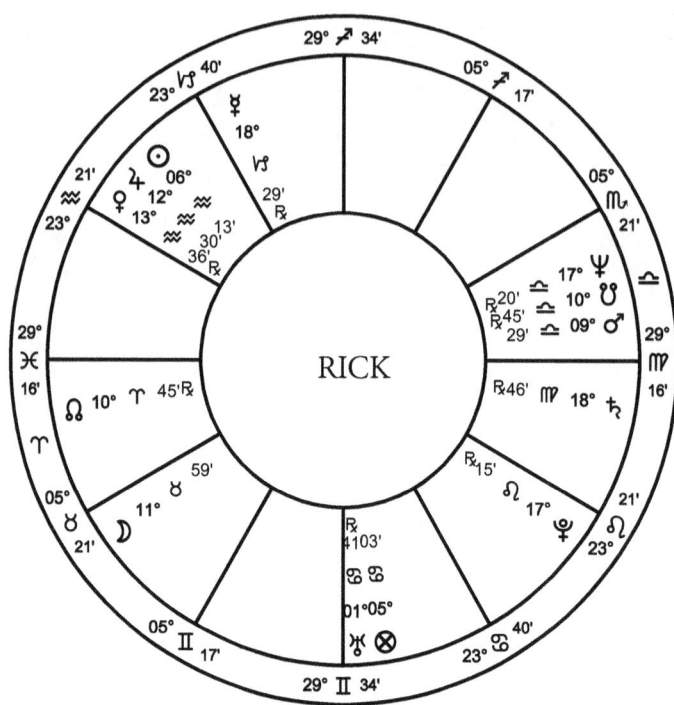

involved in molding the child to her vision of what she wants him to be. The issue with Pluto is one of control. As the child tries to establish his identity, he finds himself involved in an intense power struggle in which his chances of winning are minimal. Future relationships will be colored by control issues and fear of intimacy.

In Rick's chart, there is a T-square involving Pluto with the female planets Moon and Venus. He has a Fixed/Air temperament that fits with the Gemini 4th house. He was adopted at birth, the disruption seen in Uranus in Cancer squaring his Ascendant. His parents were born overseas and were highly intellectual. The father was a professional writer who traveled a lot. The emphasis at home was on communication, language and learning. Rick was sent to an exclusive private school where he learned French at an early age. The ruler of the 4th house in the tenth shows how the mother assumed the role of both parents since the father abdicated his role by choice and by travel.

He used the son as a buffer to keep his wife from running his life. The Grand Earth trine shows that there was no lack of material things while Rick was growing up. The mother controlled him to a large extent with money by fostering a dependency on the "good things" in life. Note the Venus/Jupiter conjunction squaring the Moon. The trine of the Moon and Saturn adds the element of distance and coldness. Rick was not able to break from his mother's control until she died when he was in his late twenties. The consequences of being raised by the Smothering Mother shows in Rick's inability to sustain an intimate emotional relationship. He quickly feels smothered and has to break away.

An important thing to note here is when there is a disturbance in the attachment process. This may come about because of the illness or death of the mother, or separation by any means which happens during the first three years of life. In this case, the neurophysiological processes of the child are affected which can lead to adult problems such as depression, anxiety disorders, panic disorders or detachment. Even short term separations have an effect but these are easily overcome once the loving mother again appears.

Trust versus Mistrust

In the Lunar period the attachment process is the foundation of the child's trust or mistrust in the environment. This concept of trust versus mistrust is the 1st stage of the psychoemotional development theory of psychoanalyst Erik Erikson. In his book, *Childhood and Society* (1950), Erikson postulated 8 Stages of Man in which the success of each stage depends on the amount of success achieved in the previous stage. Existing research based on his work has shown that early harmonious interactions between parent and child benefits the child in many ways including self-esteem, cognitive and social competence, self-control and ego-resilience. Trust basically develops from the infant and child's assurance that his environment is "dependable". The infant's signals are consistently responded to by a loving caregiver. The baby feels safe predicting that his needs will be met, he will be protected and comforted. As the child grows, the sense of trust is expanded toward other figures in his life. The child becomes more sociable through the preschool years as he interacts with peers, learning the benefits of sharing and cooperation. Expectations of the child's behavior also become part of the internal model he is building of this social system. In return, the parent takes on the role of teacher laying out the rules and limitations of the system taking into considerations the child's individual needs and capacities. The child recognizes the benefits of the system and commits to a healthy compliance with the rules. Thus a basis for a successful socialization process is established. The child's expectation that the world is a good place expands. These securely attached children tend to be more independent, perform better in school, are successful in relationships, and are less likely to develop problems such as depression and anxiety.

As seen from the previous section, when the attachment process is faulty, the sense of trust is weakened. An insecure attachment leads to a mistrust of the environment. The child experiences fear, anxiety, insecurities and a general mistrust that his needs will be met consistently or in a loving manner. In this system, the child learns to comply with rules because of fear, particularly of the loss of parental love.

Given the importance of the various processes on development of the child in this Lunar Period, it is important to note that things do not always run smoothly. There are many factors that can intervene to change the pattern such as divorce, death of a caregiver, changes in the family, even changes in parenting skills. Nor do the results of a problematical attachment have to remain permanent. Counseling or psychotherapeutic intervention during adult years can rectify many of the problems associated with these early years. It has been demonstrated that the development of trust between therapist and client is the first step toward recovery and healing. As astrologers, we can be part of this process.

Temperament, Parenting and "Goodness of Fit"

What can be learned from research in the area of temperament and parenting? The most important fact is that the earliest interactions between parent and infant affect behavioral outcomes. Two conclusions can be drawn about what is needed to enhance the child's development. First, the parents need to be sensitive to the child's signals and be flexible enough to adapt their parenting strategies to meet those needs. They need to avoid making value judgments about temperamental characteristics by labeling them in a negative way. Second, the parents need to be aware of the temperamental type characteristics of each child when structuring the environment which includes decisions about day care, timing of school entry, size and type of preschool, etc. For instance, the highly distractible school child benefits from a quiet environment with limited distractions and frequent breaks from school tasks in order to enhance achievement in learning.

Another important point made by research on those children who are more difficult to parent: acknowledgement of and advice on how to handle "difficult" children has shown to be very helpful. Avoiding labeling such as "naughty" or "bad" is important in order to prevent them from becoming self-fulfilling prophecies. As the child grows older, there is some ameliorating of characteristics such as intensity of reaction, slow adaptability, negative mood, etc. in the more moderate cases. Only in the extreme levels of the difficult temperament do these characteristics remain stable over time. However, the good news is that, even in the extreme cases, proper acceptance and handling of these children can have more positive outcomes if the parents are informed and flexible enough to adapt their parenting strategies to the child's needs. The "problem" does not stem from the child. It lies within whether or not he fits with his environment.

Astrologers can be a source for parents on how best to structure the environment, both social and physical, in order to provide the best "fit" possible.

Chapter 8

Parenting Issues

"It should always be kept in mind that what you are after with your child is not that he should learn obedience but that he should learn how to govern himself."

Unknown

The Tenth House

In Chapter 7 I discussed issues around the nurturing aspect of parenting found in the 4th house. In this chapter we'll look at the discipline issues centered in the 10th house. This house represents the child's first experience of authority. Even as an infant, the beliefs, values and parenting strategies of the parents' culture influence their responses to the child's needs. As a counselor, teacher, and astrologer, I have found it very beneficial to be familiar with parenting strategies of various cultures. Will the baby be bottle or breast fed? For how long? Will he be left to "cry it out" or picked up and held? Will a strict schedule be followed or will it be flexible based on the baby's internal schedule? When and how will toilet training be introduced? How will treatment of boys differ from that of girls?

Discipline is the responsibility of both parents, but in times gone by discipline was the father's job. This is not so true today unless the family is very traditional. With the increase in divorce, a single parent may be responsible for both nurturing and discipline aspects of parenting. The ideal scenario is when both parents are in the home, they agree on the expectations of behavior of their children and are consistent in applying consequences for breaches of those expectations. It is important to note here the difference between punishment and discipline. If a child is punished (spanked, isolated, love withdrawn, threats, etc.) he learns shame, fear and guilt. Punishing only works if the parent is standing next to the child at all times. The child learns to avoid punishment by lying, evasiveness, blaming others, or making excuses. Discipline, however, requires the parents to have appropriate expectations of the child and be consistent in carrying out consequences. When the child is young the consequences are small, such as short time out, taking a toy away, removing the child from a difficult situation. As they get older, the consequences become bigger. If the child hasn't learned by 5 or 6, it's not because they are "bad" but because parents failed to teach the child self-control and responsibility for his actions. The purpose of discipline is to help the child develop an inner structure that directs his behavior in appropriate ways, even when the parent is not present. We call that a conscience: the ability to know right from wrong.

The power the parents have lies in the child's willingness to obey because it is in his own best interest. Parents have to put in the time and energy for the child. Better to put it in when the child is young rather than later when he's grown up and is in trouble. Then it requires even more time and energy. For example, every time parents give in to the persistent child, they are robbing him of learning self-control and responsibility. The best book I know, have used, and recommend to parents is *How to Talk So Children Listen (And How to Listen So Children Will Talk)* by Adele Faber and Elaine Mazlish (1980). This book has been a best seller for more than 25 years and still going strong. They have written other books as well and have their own website. This is the best resource for parents on how to discipline their children in a positive, healthy way.

The 10th house also indicates the type of goals for achievement parents set for their children. What do the parents value most in society? What kind of behaviors will be recognized and rewarded? For example, Aries on the 10th will expect the child to be independent and competitive. Libra would expect the child to be cooperative and fair in dealing with others. The 10th house sign, its ruler and sign and house position should be carefully analyzed.

Hayden has Aries on the 10th house with the ruler, Mars, in Leo in the 1st house. He is a slow-to-warm-up child who withdraws from anything new and takes some time to adapt. Any forcefulness or anger associated with Mars is constrained by the conjunction with Saturn. While he may be expected to be independent and competitive, the square to Jupiter fosters dependency. Hayden relies on a lot of emotional support from both parents. The opposition to Neptune blurs the boundaries and makes consequences inconsistent. He eats what and when he wants. He determines his own bedtime. At times he angrily rebels (Mars inconjunct Uranus) against the lack of consistent routines which he craves. The Mars/Saturn conjunction gives him the self-discipline to succeed in school and in the one sport he excels in, Tai Kwando.

Hayden's sister, Clara, has Leo on the 10th house with ruler in Virgo in the 11th house. This ruler, like Hayden's, is also conjunct Saturn. Clara is a strongly persistent child and her frequent temper tantrums can bring out the Virgo criticism and Leo anger when the parent becomes frustrated with her. At other times, it is restrained. With both parents' Pluto on her Sun, they try to control her with reason but the opposition to Uranus shows their efforts are inconsistent. The lack of limits and boundaries is shown by the Neptune/MC opposition. The Venus on the MC shows the strong relationship to the father who is the primary caretaker. The parents both take pride in Clara's ability to express herself creatively through music and acting ability and her love of "dressing up".

Another example is the chart of a friend who has Scorpio on the 10th house cusp; the ruler, Mars, is in Pisces opposing Neptune in the 8th house. Caroline came from a poor family dominated by an angry, abusive and alcoholic father. The family was always struggling with money because of the father's drinking. There was little nurturing with the ruler of the 4th in Capricorn in the 12th house. The mother played the role of martyr and was cold, showing little affection. Pluto in the 7th house opposing the Sun/Ascendant conjunction indicates how control issues have colored her relationships, particularly with authority figures.

Family Issues and Styles

In looking at the parenting axis as a whole, we see the relationship between the nurturing, emotional support of the 4th house and the structure of rules and behavioral expectations of the 10th house. When examining issues around parenting, it should be kept in mind that these are the experiences of the child based on his/her perceptions which may or may not be aligned with reality. As we have seen, each child's unique temperament colors his response to parenting. This was brought home to me in my practice as a Marriage, Family and Child Therapist. I had the opportunity to work with three adult siblings at different times who each had parenting issues. Their descriptions of and relationships with their parents varied greatly.

Eventually I was able to work with the mother and was surprised at how much she differed from their descriptions.

The nuclear family is "an interactive and interdependent structure of individuals each of whom revolves arounds a mysterious common hub…" states Erin Sullivan in her comprehensive study *The Astrology of Family Dynamics* (2001). This excellent book provides an in-depth understanding of how families work from an astrological point of view. A must-read for anyone wanting to understand the child in the chart.

In examining the parental axis, we find different combinations of responsiveness on one hand and demandingness on the other. In each combination there are family issues that are stressed in the child's life. The aspects between the rulers give some further clues as to how these issues are resolved (soft aspects), are in conflict (hard aspects), or are in abeyance (no aspect until one appears by progression or transit). Signs and house placements give additional information. Next we look at combinations of the signs on the parenting axis for their individual themes. The signs and house placements of the rulers add subtle variations to the themes.

Aries/Libra

There are issues around identity, independence versus dependence, assertion versus accommodation. Anger and placating behavior may dominate parenting.

> **Aries 4th House**: Security is built around the idea of freedom to be oneself. The child is encouraged to explore and act independently. There is activity and energy in the home but there is also tension in the form of impatience and restlessness. There may be a lack of tenderness. Changes in residence in the early years may occur. The child may be viewed as a challenge.
>
> **Libra 4th House**: Security is built around peace and harmony. There is affection and tenderness in an environment of beauty and balance that stresses pleasing relationships.
>
> **Aries 10th House**: Achievement and discipline center around expectations of independence, leadership and competitiveness. Discipline may be interfering, martial and dominating in resolving conflicts, expressing anger with caustic remarks.
>
> **Libra 10th House**: Discipline centers around fairness and cooperation. The child is expected to be polite, tasteful, and able to see both sides of an argument. Good taste and appreciation of the arts are stressed. Parent acts as a "judge" of behavior and uses negotiation to resolve conflicts.

Taurus/Scorpio

Issues involve control and power, self-indulgence versus self-control, sensuality, sexuality, and materialism.

> **Taurus 4th House**: Security centers around affection expressed in a tactile, sensual way. Beauty of possessions along with comfort are stressed in the environment. Nurturing is patient, reliable and kind. The child may be viewed as a possession.
>
> **Scorpio 4th House**: Nurturing is tinged with strong emotions that can feel overwhelming to the child. Security becomes centered

around defense against the passion to control. Tension in the home arises from a mysterious sense of fear of the unknown.

Taurus 10th House: Achievement and discipline center around the drive to succeed. The child is expected to be honest, reliable and hard-working. Discipline may be based on monetary rewards for success and removal of same for failure. Rules are stable and consistent rather than flexible and are presented in a patient, determined manner.

Scorpio 10th House: Discipline here is meted out by a powerful presence who expects unquestioning obedience to the rules, many of which are unwritten. Achievement centers around self-mastery and the ability to "out-perform" peers. Failure can produce sarcastic criticism in return. The child learns that controlling his life is the only way to feel safe.

Gemini/Sagittarius

Parenting issues are involved with interacting, communicating, reasoning and teaching. Talking to the child is the preferred way to handle him. Goals and how they are achieved become important. Emotions are filtered through the mental processes.

Gemini 4th House: Security is built around the ability to be flexible and adaptable. Nurturing is playful but restless with an emphasis on parent/child dialogue. The environment stresses books, educational toys and learning. Child is seen as the learner. Siblings may be involved in the child's care.

Sagittarius 4th House: Security is built around space and freedom to explore. Nurturing is cheerful and optimistic with an emphasis on learning. Home environment is cultured, philosophical or religious. There is probably travel involved in the early years with an interest in nature, the outdoors and a love of animals.

Gemini 10th House: Achievement centers on reason and logic, intelligence and learning. The child is expected to be curious, flexible, and articulate. Humor and wit are rewarded along with skills in reading and writing. Discipline stems from lists of rules that are flexible as the child ages. Debate around issues is welcomed. Since friendly Gemini is sociable, exclusion from social events can act as a consequence for breaking rules.

Sagittarius 10th House: Achievement centers on learning and education which is idealistic. The child is expected to be energetic, outgoing and independent, perhaps athletic. Honesty and straight talk are expected and ignorance is not tolerated. Parent acts as a teacher using communication and reason to present the rules. Discipline here involves confinement since freedom is valued.

Cancer/Capricorn

There are issues around emotional security needs versus authority and responsibility; conditional versus unconditional love. Dependency can be an issue, either being too dependent on a parent or a parent being too dependent so that maturation and leaving home become more difficult.

Cancer 4th House: Nourishment is equated with nurturing. Nurturing is warm, affectionate, and protective. Security is built around the home and family which provides a safe structure. Early childhood experiences have great impact on the child's life because past memories are the strongest. Emotional changes in mood can have a strong impact because what is needed most is a sense of safety and tranquility. The child is seen as important love object.

Capricorn 4th House: Nurturing can be cold, routine, structured and orderly. There may be poverty or depression in the home, even neglect. There is a lack of loving support and emotional closeness. Insecurity is built into the nurturing process which leads to a distrust of others as the child grows. The child is seen as a responsibility.

Cancer 10th House: Discipline and achievement center around traditional family values. Discipline may be loving but inconsistent based on moods. The child is expected to be sensitive, receptive, domestic and home-loving, and emotionally expressive. Consequences for breaking rules may take the form of withholding food or love.

Capricorn 10th House: Achievement and discipline center around issues of responsibility, obedience and hard work. The child is expected to follow the rules which are usually rigid and inflexible over time. The child is encouraged to be reliable, cautious, respectful and to help maintain the family's public "good reputation". Discipline is of the authoritarian type which is strict and uncompromising, tinged with the "Spare the rod and spoil the child" attitude. Parent is seen as the lawgiver.

Leo/Aquarius

There are issues around closeness versus freedom; the need to love and be loved; admiration and attention can be an issue with a parent, either needing it or giving it; the child can be rewarded for "performance".

Leo 4th House: Nurturing is warm, affectionate and playful. The environment fosters creative expression, material and physical pleasures. The child is seen as an object of pride and an extension of the parent, therefore expected to look and act as a "star".

Aquarius 4th House: Nurturing may be detached or impersonal and often inconsistent. The caretaker may be absent, busy with other activities or other children. Detachment is built into the attachment process. Child is seen as a friend rather than a dependent child. Freedom to explore is encouraged.

Leo 10th House: Achievement and discipline center around the pride that comes from success. The child is expected to be ambitious, self-confident, honest and proud and often expected to achieve the unfulfilled dreams of the parent. For example, parents who didn't make it as athletes may push their sons into sports early and expect them to perform well. Discipline is meted out by a powerful authority figure who can be arrogant and demanding. Angry outbursts are not uncommon when expected results are not forthcoming. Loss of parental pride and child's pleasurable activities are threatened or applied.

Aquarius 10th House: Achievement and discipline center around the need for freedom and independence. The child is expected to be inventive, original and idealistic. He is rewarded for being intelligent, friendly, a leader who is humanitarian, for being "different" from the crowd. Discipline is erratic and unpredictable and usually involves a loss of freedom for the child. Parent can become cold and distant to the child when angered.

Virgo/Pisces

There are issues around perfection or the lack of it; codependent issues involving victim and rescuer; there can be an atmosphere of worry, negativity and dissatisfaction in the home, or a preoccupation with health and hygiene, or an emphasis on religion and sacrifice. Problems with alcoholism and drug addiction may also be present.

Virgo 4th House: Nurturing stresses orderly routines and schedules. Environment is organized, clean and hygienic or the complete opposite. The caretaker may be consumed with worry and anxiety which affects the child. Affection is rather sterile and timid and the child is seen as an object of imperfection that requires regular attention.

Pisces 4th House: Nurturing involves sensitivity to the child's needs but carelessness and confusion in responding. Boundaries may be blurred resulting in a codependent relationship between child and caretaker. The environment may be uncertain because of problems related to mental illness, alcohol or drug addiction or a sense of martyrdom.

Virgo 10th House: Achievement and discipline are colored with the idea of perfection. The child is expected to be helpful, practical, useful, thrifty and health conscious. Discipline is critical and fault-finding, never completely satisfied. Expectations of the child stress work rather than play. Consequences most likely center on loss of pleasurable activities replaced by emphasis on study and chores.

Pisces 10th House: Ideas of achievement and discipline are inconsistent. There can be an attitude of negativity and pessimism. Authority figure may be over-idealized in some way, perhaps because of absence or more attention paid to worldly affairs, such as found with physicians or ministers. The child is expected to be sensitive, idealistic or religious, self-sacrificing in service to family needs. Discipline may have a religious approach to consequences with a "this-is-done-for-your-own-good" attitude. Consequences vary and are applied inconsistently.

To illustrate the analysis of the parental axis, Joan's chart is a good example of how her early childhood shaped her adulthood. Her temperamental type is that of a slow-to-warm-up child. Her astrological type is that of Cardinal/ Earth. With the Aries/Libra parent axis there would be issues around assertion versus accommodation. Anger and placating behavior dominate parenting. Her strong Cardinality would fit with this axis except that both rulers are in Fixed signs in the elements of Fire and Water. The process of attachment was affected by some difficult aspects such as both Pluto and Saturn squaring the Ascendant. In addition, the Moon in Capricorn conjunct the South Node and Saturn in the 4th house indicate that at a deeply instinctive level Joan didn't trust her parents to care for her or to give her the security she craved.

There would also be some unconscious anger which would appear in the later developmental stages. The parents seemed to be in harmony when Joan was born (Sun trine the Moon). However, conflicts over parenting issues arose later, shown by the square aspect between the rulers of the parenting axis. The ruler of the 10th house is Mars in Scorpio in the 4th house indicating the demands and expectations of how the child should be raised dominating the nurturing process and early development. It also suggests the sexual aura of the father/

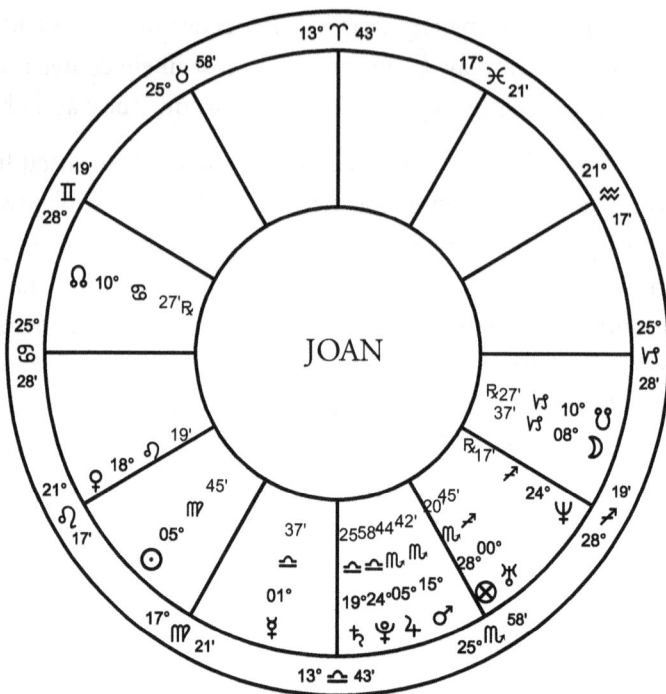

daughter relationship which made more objective observers very uncomfortable. Joan kissed him on the lips and snuggled in his lap frequently which continued throughout childhood. 4th house Pluto squaring the Ascendant shows how Joan's identity was submerged by the father's control in the relationship. Strong control can be overwhelming and fearful in a small child. Joan was demanding of her father's attention and given to frequent tantrums when she didn't get it.

Other elements in the chart added to the difficulty in Joan's course of development. Problems in relationships stem from the Wedge pattern with no oppositions lying within the Moon's Nodes. The Wedge, falling in the subjective hemisphere, increases the tendency toward introversion and the need for privacy. "Lacking in innate resources to deal with the problems," states Robert Jansky (1974, p.50), results from the Wedge pattern without the trine aspect between the boundary planets. The Moon's weak placement in Capricorn shows the tendency to shyness and seriousness. Also, being strong in the

Earth/Air elements and low in the Water element adds to the sense of detachment, a distrust of others' (and her own) emotions, and a feeling of loneliness and fear. In the square between the Moon and Mercury, Mercury in its triplicity dominates the Moon in detriment. Mercury in the 3rd house has semisquares to both Venus and Mars and is also square to Neptune. Joan has five half-siblings from the father's two previous marriages. She does not have particularly good relationships with them, especially the youngest half-sister who lived in the household when they were young. There was a serious battle between the two for father's attention.

At age 34, Joan suffers from severe depression, lack of self-esteem, poor body image, and a lack of supportive relationship. She dropped out of school early and did not establish a means of supporting herself. She has lived with her parents or maternal relations her whole life. She spends much of her time alone in her own private world.

In stark contrast to Joan's course of development, we've examined the charts of Hayden and his sister Clara throughout the book. In the case of those two, it is clear that both children, in spite of their different temperaments, have a relatively good fit with their environment. In addition, the parents are in agreement on how to handle their children, have a relaxed though often inconsistent way of running the household (in this case, the inconsistency is consistent), have provided the good nurturing required as a basis for the establishment of a sense of trust and the foundation of a secure attachment to set the children on a course of positive, healthy development which will lead to a successful adulthood. The fact that they were able to recognize the temperamental differences in their children and adapt their parenting strategies to meet the individual needs of each ensured a successful outcome for these children.

Chapter 9

Concluding Thoughts

"The child is father of the man."
                                William Wordsworth

Understanding the child's temperament is the foundation of or the context in which further analysis of the chart proceeds. The temperament of the child is present at birth. The parents respond to that temperament. The child, in turn, responds to the parents. This double-directed process continues throughout the developing years. Sometimes the process runs smoothly. Sometimes it does not. Once the astrologer understands this process, analyzing the rest of the chart can proceed along the usual lines: signs, houses, planets, aspects, patterns, "stand-outs", etc. Each astrologer has his or her own method for interpreting the horoscope, usually from an adult point of view, so I would not presume to add to that. However, I will add that every adult started out as a child. In his poem *My Heart Leaps Up When I Behold*, William Wordsworth reminds us that "The child is father of the man," and those personality traits and attitudes developed in childhood determine what the adult will be like. It might be useful for astrologers to find the child in the chart before proceeding to the interpretation of the adult chart.

To elaborate on this theme, I would like to share some of the results of more recent research studies on temperament and development. The Dunedin Multidisciplinary Health and Development Research Unit (Caspi, 2000) followed a group of 1037 children from age 3 to 21 years. The purpose of the research was to determine the influence of early temperamental differences on development over time. All of the children were born in the same year and represented all walks of life. Two outstanding facts of this research were (1) by the end of the study, 97% of the initial group were still being assessed and (2) the team consisted of participants who were able to assess the children across many domains of social and psychological functions.

The three groups of children identified through testing resemble the main temperamental types established by Thomas, Chess and Birch as follows:

1. The well-adjusted type (like the "easy type") was found to be self-confident, adapted easily and demonstrated good self-control.

2. The uncontrolled type (like the "difficult type") was impulsive, restless, negative and distractible.

3. The inhibited type (like the slow-to-warm-up type) was found to be reticent, fearful and easily upset by change.

The groups were assessed again every 2 years until age 15, then again at 18 and 21. Additional information was gathered from parents, teachers, friends, romantic partners, as well as from self-assessments by the participants. The study concluded that temperamental differences shape the course of development. The temperamental qualities were found able to predict behavior problems in childhood, personality structure at 18, the quality of interpersonal relationships at 21, the availability of social support in young adulthood, unemployment, psychiatric disorders, and criminal behavior at 21. For example, the uncontrolled and inhibited children were more likely to develop psychological disorders in the teen years than the well-adjusted children. Uncontrolled children were more likely to leave school early and were more at risk of unemployment and criminal behavior as well as conflicted relationships. There was also a difference in behaviors exhibited by the uncontrolled children and the inhibited children. Uncontrolled children were more likely to develop externalized behavior problems such as bullying, fighting, lying and disobeying. The inhibited children were more likely to develop internalizing behavior problems such as fear, worrying, crying easily and fussing.

One of the main questions arising from the study concerns how these temperamental qualities are continued and maintained over time. The answer lies within the individual's experience with his/her social environment. The interpersonal relationships with parents, siblings, teachers and significant others helps maintain the process of interaction in a continuous manner that reinforces the responses on both sides. Therefore, continuity of behavioral patterns is more likely than that of change.

Does this mean that change is not possible? No, definitely not. Change can occur naturally or by planned intervention. When parents are informed and capable of changing their parenting strategies, change in the behavior of the child can occur. With emotional support and encouragement, inhibited children can learn to adapt more rapidly and successfully. When uncontrolled children are given consistent, firm boundaries along with warm, loving care, they can gradually master self-control.

Another important area for discussion is the effect of temperamental differences on the child's success or failure in school. (Keough, 2003). Research on this topic was part of the Fullerton Longitudinal Project (Guerin et al, 2003) which studied 130 infants and their families beginning at one year of age with continuous assessment over 17 years. Some of the interesting findings included:

1. "Higher grades in high school is predicted in early infancy by a stable pattern of persistence/attention span and adaptability." (p.178) It should also be noted that lack of these traits was strongly related to what teachers considered "behavior problems". "Teachers equate high levels of persistence, adaptability, positive mood, and low levels of activity and distractibility with school achievement." (p.178)

2. Children with extreme levels of the characteristics of the "difficult child" type suffered from conflict in the home where they had "less verbal and emotional interaction, received fewer opportunities for a variety of stimulation and were more likely to be punished physically." (p.284) These children showed more externalized problems such as

bullying, lying and defiance of authority which would worsen over time.

3. The slow-to-warm-up children suffered "less maternal pride, affection and warmth, less variety in stimulation and more physical punishment." (p.281) These children tended to develop internalized problems such as anxiety, depression and avoidance.

There is a growing list of research studies that continue to reinforce the importance of taking the temperament of children into consideration when discussing home and school environments. The concept of "goodness of fit" has been thoroughly validated. Temperamental characteristics of children affects their social relationships, socially appropriate behavior, and academic success.

The purpose of this book has been to inform professional astrologers on the importance of determining the temperament of the child (in the modern sense) from the natal chart. My hope is that, in helping parents understand the individual needs of their children, they will be able to create the kind of environment which will produce the "best fit" and thus the best possible behavioral outcomes. That way, everybody is happy!

Appendix A

Parent Questionnaire

Name of child _____

Date of Birth _____   Time of Birth _____

Place of Birth (City, State) _____

Mother's Birthdate _____

Father's Birthdate _____

Home Information
Persons living in the home and relationship to the child: (Please list)

Child's position in the family: (Please circle)   1 2 3 4 5 6 7 8

Number of brothers: _____   Ages _____

Number of sisters: _____   Ages: _____

Check one:
Both parents in home? _____

Parents separated or divorced? _____   Since? _____

Step-Parent in the home? _____

Who cared for the child other than the mother? (Please list)

Circumstances of Birth
Special conditions at delivery:

Natural Birth _____   Caesarian (surgical) _____
Induced labor _____   Breech _____
Forceps used _____   Other _____

Any special problems at birth such as cord around the neck or RH blood requiring blood transfusion?   _____

Any birth defects such as hernia?   _____

Health History
Any special problems such as allergies, hearing or eyesight problems?
_____

Please list all childhood diseases the child has had, such as measles. Also list any serious illness, surgery, or broken bones or any other problems the child has had and about what age.
_____
_____
_____

Please list child's habits such as nail biting, ear pulling, thumb sucking etc.
_____

Have there been any speech problems such as stuttering?
_____

Does the child have any special fears such
as fear of the dark or animals? (Please list)
_____

Please explain the form of discipline used at home such as spanking, scolding, isolation.
_____

Infant's Behaviour Before Age Two

Walked at what age? _____ Began talking at what age? _____

What was the baby like when you first brought him/her home?
_____

How much did your baby move around? (Check one)
- _____ Very active (constant motion, wriggled a lot, hard to dress, hard to keep covers on)
- _____ Not very active (quiet, stayed where placed, easy to dress)
- _____ Average   (activity level varied)

How did this child respond to new situations? For example, did it take him/her a long time to adjust to a bath, a new food, or a new person?
- _____ Adjusted quickly
- _____ Took a long time
- _____ Average

How would you describe the baby's sensitivity to noises, heat and cold, tastes, textures?
- _____ Highly sensitive (for example, woke to the slightest noise)
- _____ Low (for example, can sleep through anything)
- _____ Average

Did the baby respond to things in a quiet way or did he/she react strongly? For example, did he let his pleasure or displeasure at something be known by screaming or whimpering?
- _____ Reacted strongly
- _____ Reacted slightly
- _____ Average

If the baby is involved in an activity such as sucking a bottle, could he/she be distracted easily by a sound or another person?
- _____ Highly distractible
- _____ Not distracted
- _____ Average

Could the baby stay involved in an activity for a long time or did he tire of it quickly?
_____ Attention span long
_____ Attention span short
_____ Average

If the child couldn't accomplish something easily, did he/she give up trying or keep at it?
_____ Gave up quickly
_____ Persisted for sometime
_____ Average

Overall, did the baby seem fairly happy and content most of the time or was he/she more often irritable and fussy?
_____ Happy most of the time
_____ irritable, cranky a lot
_____ Average

How did the child respond to new situations, eagerly or shyly?
_____ Wanted to explore and try things
_____ Needed encouragement from adult
_____ Tended to hang back for a time
_____ Cried

Appendix B

Student Observations

Intensity of Reactions

Name	Very Intense	Average	Low Intensity	Date

High Intensity: Screams, shouts, tantrums, loud laughter
Average: Smiles, chuckles, whines, pouts
Low Intensity: Shows little emotion

Appendix C

Worksheets

Worksheet #1: Astrological Type

NAME   **DATA**

Fill in blanks with appropriate signs. Add up points for elements and qualities.

PLANET	SIGN	POINTS	ELEMENT TOTALS	
Sun		20	Fire	
Sun Ruler		20	Earth	
Moon		15	Air	
Ascendant		10	Water	
Asc. Ruler		10	**Total**	100
Mercury		5		
Venus		5	**QUALITY TOTALS**	
Mars		5	Cardinal	
Jupiter		4	Fixed	
Saturn		3	Mutable	
Uranus		1	**Total**	100
Neptune		1		
Pluto		1	**ASTROLOGICAL TYPE**	
Total		100		

Lack of: Over-emphasis on:

COMPATIBLE COMBINATIONS   **INCOMPATIBLE COMBINATIONS**
Water/Earth: Air/Water: Water/Fire:
Air/Fire: Air/Earth: Earth/Fire:

QUALITY OF MOOD
Check one according to levels of Fire/Air (over 65), balanced (35-65), Water/Earth (over 65)

Positive   Balanced   Negative

Worksheet #2: Approach/Withdrawal

NAME   DATA

Examine the chart and assign points as follows:

Points	Approach		Withdrawal	
30	Positive Mood	_____	Negative Mood	_____
25	Fire or Air Asc	_____	Earth or Water Asc	_____
20	Asc. Ruler Fire/Air	_____	Asc. Ruler Earth/Water	_____
15	Jupiter conj. Asc.	_____	Saturn conj. Asc.	_____
10	Jupiter Asp. Asc.	_____	Saturn Asp. Asc.	_____
100	**Total**	_____	**Total**	_____

Notes: Compare the totals in terms of Low (0-35), Balanced (35-65), or High (65-100). To add more information and clarification, examine the decanates with their rulers, and the dwads. In addition, note the adaptability level in comparison; for example a child with high level of withdrawal may have sufficient adaptability to take less time to overcome his/her initial response of withdrawal than a child with a high level of withdrawal and a very low level of adaptability.

Worksheet #3: Adaptability

NAME   DATA

From Worksheet #1, assign points to those elements and qualities over 25 as follows:

Points	Elements & Qualities	
30	Mutability (25+)	___
20	Cardinality (25+)	___
15	Air (25+)	___
15	Fire (25+)	___
10	Water (25+)	___
10	Earth (25+)	___
	Total	___

Notes: (Examine the total in terms of Low (0-35), Balanced (35-65) or High (65-100)

Worksheet #4: Intensity of Reaction

NAME   DATA

Examine the chart and assign points as follows:

Points	Aspects	
30	Moon aspects to Mars	_____
20	Mars aspects to Asc.	_____
20	Moon aspects to Asc.	_____
15	Moon in Aries	_____
10	Moon in 1st House	_____
5	Jupiter aspects to Moon, Mars or Asc.	_____
100	**Total**	_____

Notes: Examine the total in terms of Low (0-35), Balanced (35-65), or High (65-100). Add more information from the Incompatible Combinations from Worksheet #1)

Worksheet #5: Distractability and Persistence

NAME   DATA

Distractability

Examine the chart and assign points as follows:

Points Factors
30   Mutability Predominance (from Worksheet #1)   _____
25   Air/Fire Predominance (from Worksheet #1)   _____
20   Mercury conjunct the Ascendant   _____
15   Mercury aspects to Jupiter, Mars, Neptune   _____
10   Mercury in Gemini, Sagittarius, Aries, Pisces, Virgo _____
        Total   _____

Notes: Examine the total in terms of Low (0-35), Balanced (35-65), or High (65-100).

Persistence

Examine the chart and assign points as follows:

Points Factors
30   Fixity Predominance (from Worksheet #1)   _____
25   Earth/Water Predominance (from worksheet #1)   _____
20   Mercury aspects to Saturn, Uranus, Pluto   _____
15   Mars aspects to Saturn, Uranus, Pluto   _____
10   Mercury in Taurus, Cancer, Leo, Libra, Scorpio,
        Capricorn or Aquarius   _____
        Total   _____

Notes: Examine the totals in terms of Low (0-35), Balanced (35-65, or High (65-100).

Worksheet #6: Activity Levels

NAME   DATA

High Activity Level

Examine the chart and assign points as follows:

Points	Factors	
30	Mars aspects to Ascendant	_____
25	Mars in Aries, Gemini, Sagittarius	_____
20	Mars aspects to Sun, Jupiter, Uranus	_____
15	Sun in Aries or Sagittarius	_____
10	Sun aspects to Jupiter	_____
	Total	

Notes: Score below 50 is normal activity level; above 50 is high activity level.

Low Activity Level

Examine the chart and assign points as follows:

Points	Factors	
30	Mars in Leo, Scorpio, Taurus, Cancer, Pisces	_____
25	Neptune aspects to the Ascendant	_____
20	Saturn aspects to the Ascendant	_____
15	Mars aspects to Neptune, Saturn	_____
10	Bowl Pattern	_____
	Total	_____

Notes: Score below 50 falls in normal activity level; above 50 is low activity level.

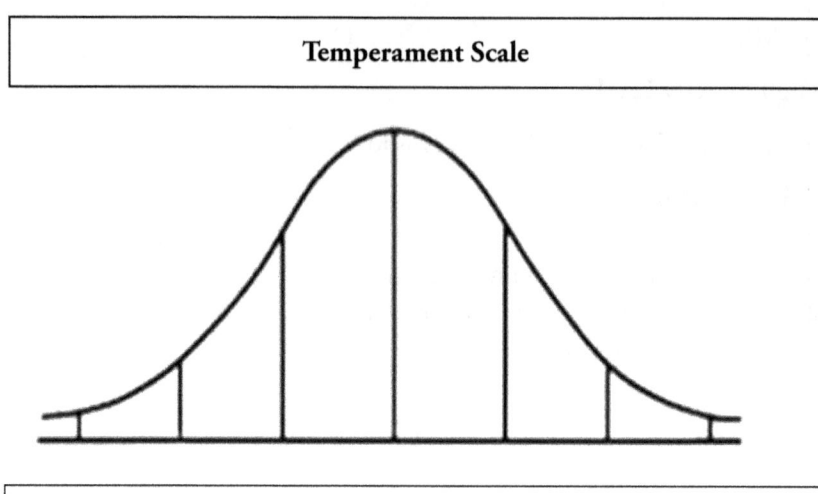

Appendix D

Temperament Assessment Scale

ACTIVITY LEVEL	highly active, always seems to be "on the go"	1 2 3 4 5 6 7	calm and content, inactive most of the time
ADAPTABILITY	adapts easily to change	1 2 3 4 5 6 7	does not adapt easily to change
REGULARITY	eating, sleeping, and bathroom habits are regular	1 2 3 4 5 6 7	eating, sleeping, and bathroom habits are irregular
SENSITIVITY	highly sensitive to pain, sounds, light, and temperature	1 2 3 4 5 6 7	not overly sensitive to pain, sounds, light, and temperature
DISTRACTIBILITY	easily distracted, unable to ignore distractions	1 2 3 4 5 6 7	highly focused, not easily distracted
MOOD	overall positive mood, usually pleasant and happy	1 2 3 4 5 6 7	overall negative mood, often angry, cries often
PERSISTENCE	sticks with projects until they are done, doesn't give up	1 2 3 4 5 6 7	does not stick with projects until they are done, gives up easily
INTENSITY	emotional reactions are intense, even exaggerated	1 2 3 4 5 6 7	emotional reactions are mild, low-key
APPROACH/ WITHDRAWAL	willing to try new things, comfortable in social situations	1 2 3 4 5 6 7	unwilling to try new things, withdraws in social situations

Bibliography

Ainsworth, M.D.S., Blehar, M.C., Waters, E., & Wall, S. *Patterns of Attachment*. Erlbaum, 1978.

Arroyo, Stephen. *Astrology, Karma and Transformation*. CRCS Publications, 1978.

———, *Astrology, Psychology, and the Four Elements*. CRCS publications, 1975.

Bater, J.E. "Adjustment style in childhood as a product of parenting and temperament." In Wachs, T.D., & Kohnstamm, G.A. (Eds.), *Temperament in Context*. Erlbaum, 2001.

Bowlby, John. *Attachment*. Basic Books, 1969.

Buss, A.H. & Plomin, R. *A Temperament Theory of Personality Development*. Wiley, 1975.

Caspi, Avshalom. "The Child is Father of the Man: Personality Continuities from Childhood to Adulthood." *Journal of Personality & Social Psychology*, 2000, Vol. 78, No.1, 158-172.

"DifferentKids/Different Temperaments." <centerforparentingeducation.org> Library of Articles: Child Development. Accessed 8/16/16.

Dobbyns, Zipporah. *Finding the Person in the Horoscope*. I.A. Publications, 1973.

Epstein, Herman T. "The Roles of Brain in Human Cognitive Development." 28 Feb 2013. www.brainstages.net

Erikson, Erik. *Childhood and Society*. W.W. Norton,1950.

Faber, Adele & Mazlish, Elaine. *How to Talk So Children Will Listen (& How to Listen So Children Will Talk)*. Rawson Associates, 1950.

Goldsmith, H.H., Bradshaw, D.L., & Riesee-Danner, L.A. "Temperament as a Potential Developmentsl Influence on Attachment." In *New Directions for Child Development*, pp.5-34. March, 1986.

Greenbaum, Dorian G. *Temperament: Astrology's Forgotten Key*. The Wessex Astrologer, 2005.

Guerin, D.W., Goottfried, A.W., Oliver, P.H. & Thomas, C.W. *Temperament: Infancy through Adolescence*. Plenum Publishers, 2003.

Hansen, Cornelia. "Child and Parent." In McEvers, Joan (Ed.), *Web of Relationships*. Llewellyn Publications, 1992.

Jansky, R.C. *Planetary Patterns*. Astro-Analytic Publications, 1974.

Jones, Marc E. *Essentials of Astrological Analysis*. Trefoil Publications, 1960.

Kagan, Jerome & Snidman, N. *The Long Shadow of Temperament*. Belknap Press of Harvard University Press, 2004.

Keogh, Barbara K. *Temperament in the classroom*. Brookes Publishing, 2003.

Main, Mary & Solomon, Judith. "Discovery of an insecure disoriented attachment." In Brazelton, T., & Youngman, M., *Affective Development in Infancy*. Ablex, 1986.

Makransky, Bob. "Mental Chemistry in the Birth Chart." *The Mountain Astrologer*, Issue #98, Aug/Sept. 2001: 73-79.

Marks, Tracy. *How to Handle Your T-Square*. Sagittarius Rising, 1979.

McClowry, Sandra G., Rodriguez, Eileen T., & Koslowitz, Robin. "Temperament-Based Intervention: Re-examining Goodness of Fit.": 2Jun2008.<nebi.nlm.nih..gov/pmc/articles.

Munkasey, Michael. *The Astrological Thesaurus*. Llewellyn Worldwide, 1993.

Pines, Maya. "Why Some Three-Year-Olds Get A's – and Some Get C's." In Anderson, R.H., & Shane, H.G. (Eds.), *As the Twig is Bent*. Houghton Mifflin, 1971.

Richters, J.E. & Waters, E. 1991 www.psychology.sunyb.edu/attachment/online/Richters_Waters. pdf

Rothbart, Mary K. "Temperament and Development." In Kohnstamm G.A., Bates J.E., & Rothbart M.K. (Eds.), *Temperament and Childhood*. (pp.187-247) Wiley, 1989.

Sanson, Ann & Rothbart, Mary K. "Child Temperament and Parenting." <Bowdoin.edu/~sputnam/rothbart-temperament-questionnaires/cv/publications/pdf/1995

Santrock, John W. *Child Development*, 10th ed. McGraw-Hill, 2004.

Scofield, Bruce. *The Circuitry of the Self.* One Reed Publications, 2001.

Sullivan, Erin. *The Astrology of Family Dynamics.* Weiser Books, 2001.

Thomas, A., Chess, Stella, & Birch, Herbert, G. *Origins & Evolution of Behavior Disorders.* Brunner/Mazel, 1984.

Thomas, A., & Chess, S. *Temperament in Clinical Practice.* Guilford Press, 1986.
_____, *Goodness of Fit.* Brunner/Mazel, 1999.

VanDenBoom, D.C. "Neonatal Irritability & the Development of Attachment." In Kohnstamm, G.A., Bates, J.E., & Rothbart, M.K. (Eds.), *Temperament in Childhood.* Wiley, 1989.

Zentner, Marcel, and Bates, John E. "Child Temperament: An Integrative Review of Concepts, Research Programs, and Measures." *European Journal of Developmental Science*, 2003, vol.2 no. 1-2, pp. 7-37. <inige,ch/tapse/emotion/tests/temperament/publications/ejda_02_o1_zentner.pdf>

Other Titles from The Wessex Astrologer
www.wessexastrologer.com

Martin Davis
Astrolocality Astrology: A Guide to What it is and How to Use it
From Here to There: An Astrologer's Guide to Astromapping

Wanda Sellar
The Consultation Chart
An Introduction to Medical Astrology
An Introduction to Decumbiture

Geoffrey Cornelius
The Moment of Astrology

Darrelyn Gunzburg
Life After Grief: An Astrological Guide to Dealing with Grief
AstroGraphology: The Hidden Link between your Horoscope and your Handwriting

Paul F. Newman
Declination: The Steps of the Sun
Luna: The Book of the Moon

Deborah Houlding
The Houses: Temples of the Sky

Dorian Geiseler Greenbaum
Temperament: Astrology's Forgotten Key

Howard Sasportas
The Gods of Change

Patricia L. Walsh
Understanding Karmic Complexes

M. Kelly Hunter
Living Lilith: the Four Dimensions of the Cosmic Feminine

Barbara Dunn
Horary Astrology Re-Examined

Deva Green
Evolutionary Astrology

Jeff Green
Pluto Volume 1: The Evolutionary Journey of the Soul
Pluto Volume 2: The Evolutionary Journey of the Soul Through Relationships
Essays on Evolutionary Astrology (ed. by Deva Green)

Dolores Ashcroft-Nowicki and Stephanie V. Norris
The Door Unlocked: An Astrological Insight into Initiation

Greg Bogart
Astrology and Meditation: The Fearless Contemplation of Change

Henry Seltzer
The Tenth Planet: Revelations from the Astrological Eris

Ray Grasse
Under a Sacred Sky: Essays on the Practice and Philosophy of Astrology

Martin Gansten
Primary Directions

Joseph Crane
Astrological Roots: The Hellenistic Legacy
Between Fortune and Providence

Bruce Scofield
Day-Signs: Native American Astrology from Ancient Mexico

Komilla Sutton
The Essentials of Vedic Astrology
The Lunar Nodes: Crisis and Redemption
Personal Panchanga: The Five Sources of Light
The Nakshatras: the Stars Beyond the Zodiac

Anthony Louis
The Art of Forecasting using Solar Returns

Oscar Hofman
Classical Medical Astrology

Bernadette Brady
Astrology, A Place in Chaos
Star and Planet Combinations

Richard Idemon
The Magic Thread
Through the Looking Glass

Nick Campion
The Book of World Horoscopes

Judy Hall
Patterns of the Past
Karmic Connections
Good Vibrations
The Soulmate Myth: A Dream Come True or Your Worst Nightmare?
The Book of Why: Understanding your Soul's Journey
Book of Psychic Development

Neil D. Paris
Surfing your Solar Cycles

Michele Finey
The Sacred Dance of Venus and Mars

David Hamblin
The Spirit of Numbers

Dennis Elwell
Cosmic Loom

Bob Makransky
Planetary Strength
Planetary Hours
Planetary Combination

Petros Eleftheriadis
Horary Astrology: The Practical Guide to Your Fate

Nicola Smuts-Allsop
Fertility Astrology: A Modern Medieval Textbook

About the Author

Since receiving her Master's Degree in Early Childhood Development at the California State University at Northridge, Cornelia Hansen has been a pre-school Director and Los Angeles Children's Center teacher. In 1982 she received a second Master's Degree from Antioch University in Clinical Psychology. She was on staff of the Hollywood Counseling Center for four years while working toward her license as a Marriage, Family and Child Therapist. While there, she taught "Mommy & Me" and parenting skills classes. She was in private practice with Encino Psychological Associates for seventeen years. She studied astrology with Joan McEvers and Marion March through Aquarius Workshops and wrote a column for their magazine "Aspects" for several years. Her chapter "Parent and Child" was included in *Web of Relationships* edited by Joan McEvers for Llewellyn Publications in 1992. As a member of AFA, her research article "Identifying Astrological Signatures of Modern Temperamental Components for Use in Working with Children's Charts" was published in AFA's Research Journal Volume 18. At present she is teaching classes for Kepler College on Counseling with Parents.

www.ingramcontent.com/pod-product-compliance
Lightning Source LLC
Chambersburg PA
CBHW070546090426
42735CB00013B/3089